PATHWAYS

SECOND EDITION

Listening, Speaking, and Critical Thinking

PAUL MACINTYRE

NATIONAL GEOGRAPHIC

LEARNING

Australia • Brazil • Mexico • Singapore • United Kingdom • United States

NATIONAL GEOGRAPHIC
L E A R N I N G

Pathways 4A: Listening, Speaking, and Critical Thinking, 2nd Edition

Paul MacIntyre

Publisher: Sherrise Roehr

Executive Editor: Laura Le Dréan

Managing Editor: Jennifer Monaghan

Associate Development Editor: Lisl Bove

Director of Global and U.S. Marketing: Ian Martin

Product Marketing Manager: Tracy Bailie

Media Research: Leila Hishmeh

Senior Director, Production: Michael Burggren

Manager, Production: Daisy Sosa

Content Project Manager: Mark Rzeszutek

Senior Digital Product Manager: Scott Rule

Manufacturing Planner: Mary Beth Hennebury

Interior and Cover Design: Brenda Carmichael

Art Director: Brenda Carmichael

Composition: MPS North America LLC

For product information and technology assistance, contact us at
Cengage Learning Customer & Sales Support, cengage.com/contact

For permission to use material from this text or product,
submit all requests online at **cengage.com/permissions**
Further permissions questions can be emailed to
permissionrequest@cengage.com

Split 4A ISBN-13: 978-1-337-56243-0
Split 4A + Online Workbook: 978-1-337-56261-4

National Geographic Learning
20 Channel Center Street
Boston, MA 02210
USA

National Geographic Learning, a Cengage Learning Company, has a mission to bring the world to the classroom and the classroom to life. With our English language programs, students learn about their world by experiencing it. Through our partnerships with National Geographic and TED Talks, they develop the language and skills they need to be successful global citizens and leaders.

Locate your local office at **international.cengage.com/region**

Visit National Geographic Learning online at **NGL.Cengage.com/ELT**
Visit our corporate website at **www.cengage.com**

Printed in China
Print Number: 03   Print Year: 2019

Contents

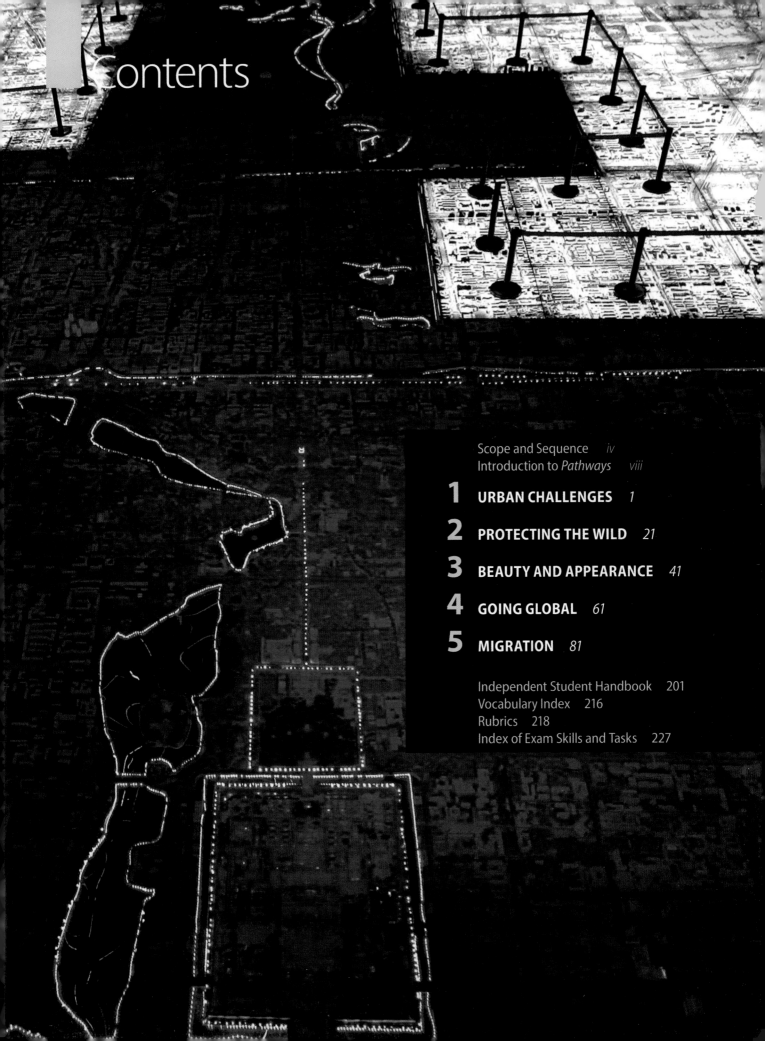

Scope and Sequence

Speaking & Presentation	Vocabulary	Grammar & Pronunciation	Critical Thinking
• Signaling Additional Aspects of a Topic • Presenting in Pairs **Lesson Task** Evaluating the Impact of Tourism **Final Task** Presenting a Problem and Solutions	Word Families: Suffixes	• Passive Voice • Linking with Word-Final *t*	**Focus:** Predicting Analyzing Visuals, Applying, Evaluating, Making Inferences, Organizing Ideas, Reflecting
• Responding to an Argument **Lesson Task** Discussing Environmental Impact **Final Task** A Debate on Wild Animals in Zoos	Two-Part Verbs with *Out*	• Essential Adjective Clauses • Saying and Linking *–s* Endings	**Focus:** Evaluating Arguments in a Debate Analyzing, Analyzing a Chart, Applying, Evaluating, Making Inferences, Predicting, Reflecting
• Paraphrasing • Preparing Visuals for Display **Lesson Task** Conducting a Survey **Final Task** A Presentation about Fashion Trends	Suffix *-ive*	• Tag Questions • Intonation for Clarification	**Focus:** Interpreting a Bar Graph Analyzing, Applying, Evaluating, Interpreting, Organizing Ideas, Predicting, Reflecting
• Defining Terms • Managing Nervousness **Lesson Task** Role-Playing a Job Interview **Final Task** Evaluating a Social Media Platform	Using Collocations	• Gerund Phrases • Saying Parentheticals	**Focus:** Evaluating Analyzing, Applying, Interpreting a Graph, Interpreting a Map, Interpreting Visuals, Organizing Ideas, Ranking, Reflecting
• Approximating • Handling Audience Questions **Lesson Task** Discussing Family Origins **Final Task** A Pair Presentation on Animal Migration	Suffixes *–ant* and *–ist*	• Modals of Past Possibility • Linking with *You* or *Your*	**Focus:** Distinguishing Fact from Theory Applying, Evaluating, Interpreting a Map, Making Inferences, Organizing Ideas, Reflecting, Synthesizing

Introduction to *Pathways*

***Pathways* Listening, Speaking, and Critical Thinking, Second Edition**

uses compelling National Geographic stories, photos, video, and
infographics to bring the world to the classroom. Authentic, relevant
content and carefully sequenced lessons engage learners while
equipping them with the skills needed for academic success.

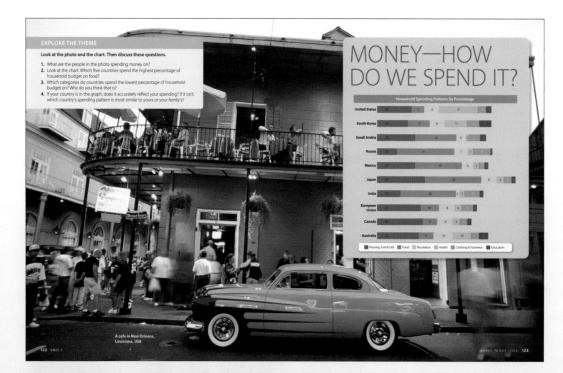

A cafe in New Orleans, Louisiana, USA

Explore the Theme
provides a visual
introduction to
the unit, engaging
learners academically
and encouraging
them to share ideas
about the unit theme.

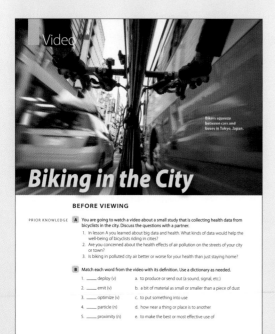

Bikers squeeze between cars and buses in Tokyo, Japan.

Biking in the City

BEFORE VIEWING

PRIOR KNOWLEDGE **A** You are going to watch a video about a small study that is collecting health data from bicyclists in the city. Discuss the questions with a partner.

1. In lesson A you learned about big data and health. What kinds of data would help the well-being of bicyclists riding in cities?
2. Are you concerned about the health effects of air pollution on the streets of your city or town?
3. Is biking in polluted city air better or worse for your health than just staying home?

B Match each word from the video with its definition. Use a dictionary as needed.

1. _____ deploy (v)   a. to produce or send out (a sound, signal, etc.)
2. _____ emit (v)   b. a bit of material as small or smaller than a piece of dust
3. _____ optimize (v)   c. to put something into use
4. _____ particle (n)   d. how near a thing or place is to another
5. _____ proximity (n)   e. to make the best or most effective use of

LISTENING FOR **B** 2.7 Listen to a podcast about augmented reality (AR). Check (✓) the two main
MAIN IDEAS ideas the speakers discuss.

1. ☐ AR is a useful technology with many different applications.
2. ☐ AR's popularity has contributed to the widespread use of portable devices.
3. ☐ AR is useful when deciding which pieces of furniture to purchase.
4. ☐ AR facilitates the globalization of culture through popular games.
5. ☐ Pokémon Go's popularity has unquestionably benefited local economies.

NEW Integrated listening and speaking activities help **prepare
students for standardized tests** such as IELTS and TOEFL.

UPDATED *Video* sections use relevant National
Geographic **video clips** to give learners another
perspective on the unit theme and further practice of
listening and critical thinking skills.

Listening Skills

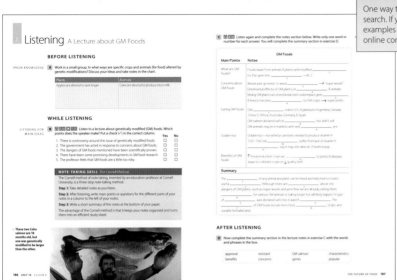

NEW *Vocabulary Skills* help students develop essential word building tools such as understanding collocations, word forms, and connotation.

Listening passages incorporate a variety of listening types such as podcasts, lectures, interviews, and conversations.

NEW *Slide shows* for selected listening passages integrate text and visuals to give learners a more authentic listening experience.

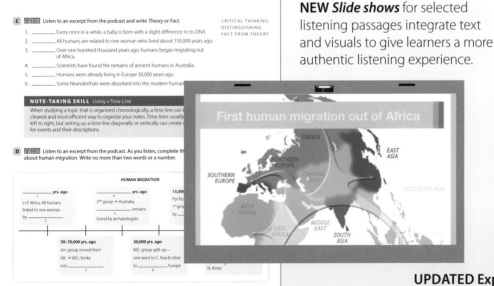

UPDATED Explicit listening and note-taking skill instruction and practice prepares students to listen and take notes in academic settings.

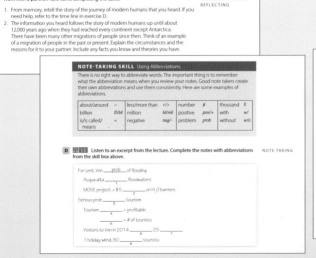

Speaking and Presentation Skills

Speaking lessons guide learners from controlled practice to a final speaking task while reinforcing speaking skills, grammar for speaking, and key pronunciation points.

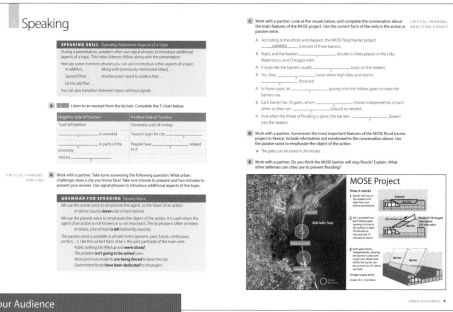

PRESENTATION SKILL Engaging Your Audience

Here are some suggestions to help you engage your audience.

- At the beginning of your presentation, ask some questions that can be answered by a show of hands.
- As appropriate during your presentation, ask for one or more volunteers to assist you or to provide an example for a point.
- Focus on how the points you are making can benefit your audience. When you do, check if they agree.
- Use rhetorical questions to encourage your audience to think about something, to invite them to agree with you, or to ask questions you think your audience would like to ask.

Presentation skills such as starting strong, using specific details, making eye contact, pausing, and summarizing, help learners develop confidence and fluency in communicating ideas.

A **Final Task** allows learners to consolidate their understanding of content, language and skills as they collaborate on an academic presentation.

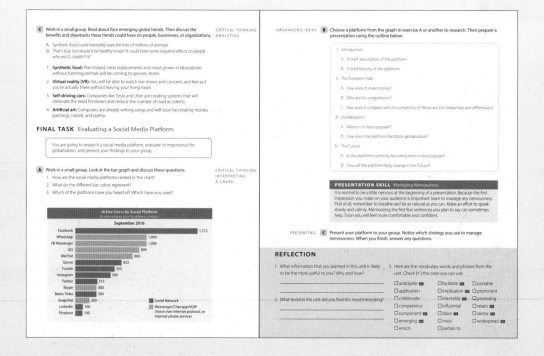

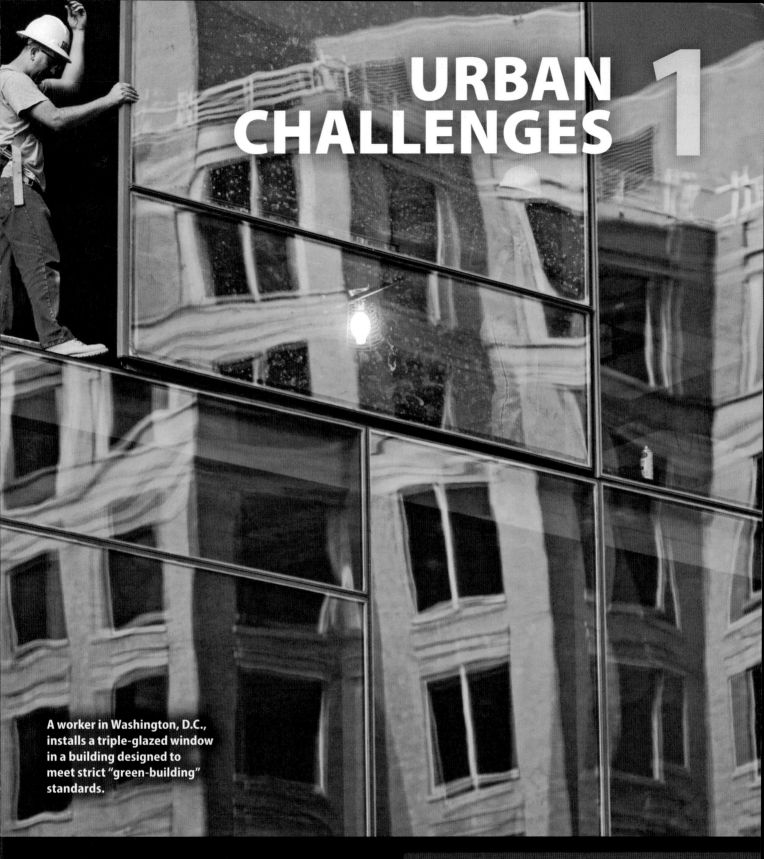

URBAN CHALLENGES 1

A worker in Washington, D.C., installs a triple-glazed window in a building designed to meet strict "green-building" standards.

ACADEMIC SKILLS

LISTENING	Understanding the Introduction to a Lecture
	Using Abbreviations
SPEAKING	Signaling Additional Aspects of a Topic
	Linking with Word-Final *t*
CRITICAL THINKING	Predicting

THINK AND DISCUSS

1 What challenge are green buildings intended to solve? In addition to windows, in what other ways can buildings be made "green"?

2 Would you move to a city that is dealing with challenges such as overcrowding? Explain.

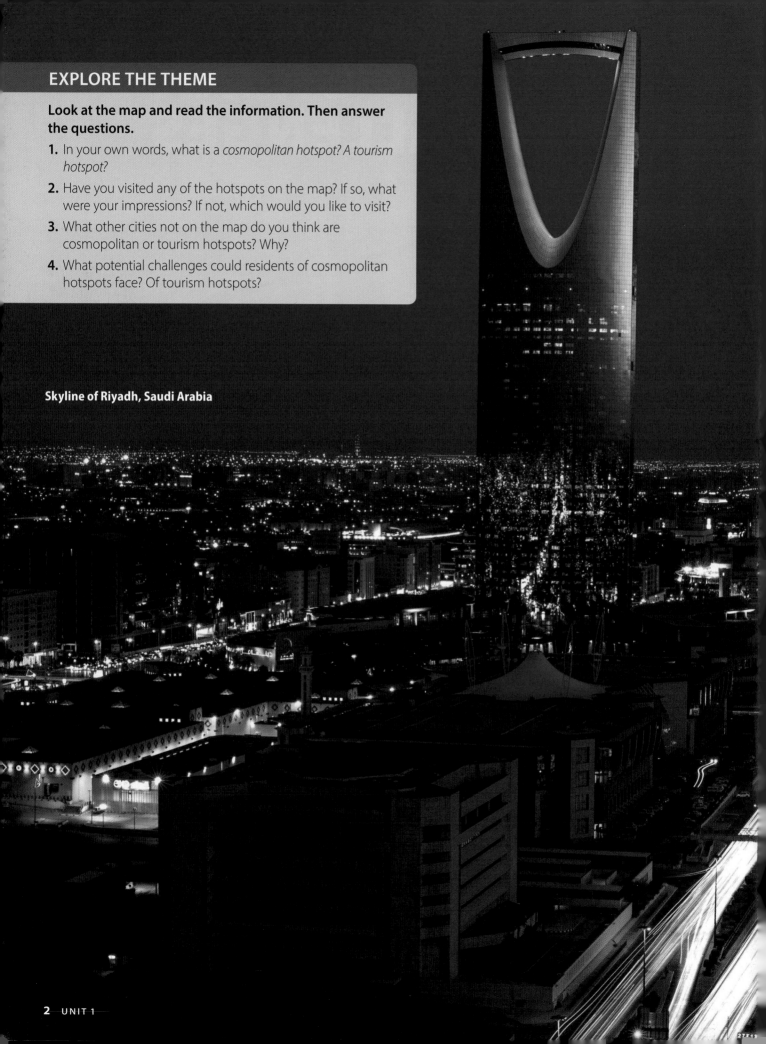

EXPLORE THE THEME

Look at the map and read the information. Then answer the questions.

1. In your own words, what is a *cosmopolitan hotspot? A tourism hotspot?*

2. Have you visited any of the hotspots on the map? If so, what were your impressions? If not, which would you like to visit?

3. What other cities not on the map do you think are cosmopolitan or tourism hotspots? Why?

4. What potential challenges could residents of cosmopolitan hotspots face? Of tourism hotspots?

Skyline of Riyadh, Saudi Arabia

WORLD CITIES: HOTSPOTS

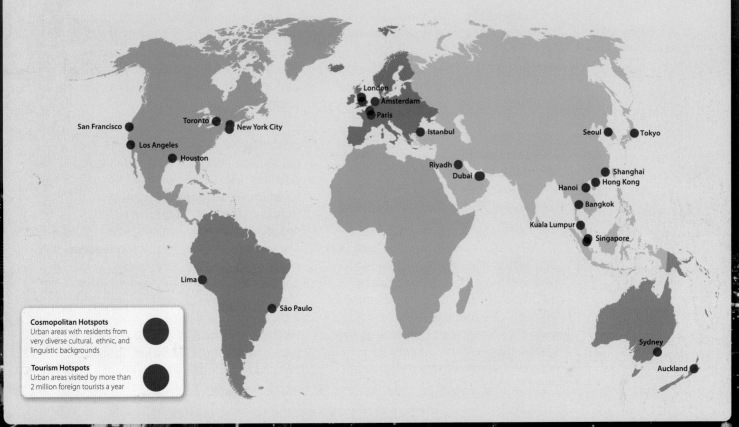

Cosmopolitan Hotspots
Urban areas with residents from very diverse cultural, ethnic, and linguistic backgrounds

Tourism Hotspots
Urban areas visited by more than 2 million foreign tourists a year

San Francisco
Los Angeles
Houston
Toronto
New York City
Lima
São Paulo
London
Amsterdam
Paris
Istanbul
Riyadh
Dubai
Seoul
Tokyo
Shanghai
Hong Kong
Hanoi
Bangkok
Kuala Lumpur
Singapore
Sydney
Auckland

A Vocabulary

A 🎧 **1.2** Read and listen to the information. Notice each word in **blue** and think about its meaning.

URBAN CHALLENGES

Today's urban areas face a variety of challenges. One challenge is a **scarcity** of land for housing. To address this problem, some residents of Tokyo, Japan, have found a unique solution: they are having homes constructed on pieces of land as small as 344 square feet (32 square meters). These "micro-homes" allow residents to live close to central Tokyo and are much more **affordable** than traditional homes in that area. Despite their size, many micro-homes have several floors and big windows that **maximize** sunlight.

Many urban areas also suffer from poor air quality due to pollution and smog.[1] What can these cities do to **regulate** the amount of chemicals from cars and factories? One **innovative** solution has been developed by an Italian company: smog-eating cement. The cement contains a substance that converts pollution into harmless chemicals that are then washed off roadways when it rains. The smog-eating material has also been effectively used in roof tiles in Los Angeles, California, where air-pollution control is **prioritized**.

Another urban challenge is finding creative ways to build public parks, gardens, and outdoor areas when space is limited. In 2002, the city of New York, for example, **authorized** a project to transform the High Line, an unused railroad line, into an elevated urban park. The **funds** necessary for this **renovation** project were provided through donations, and it was money well spent. The High Line has become one of the most inviting public spaces in the city. Visitors can **stroll** through the gardens, relax on the sundeck, or attend public art exhibits and special events.

[1] **smog** (n): a combination of smoke and fog that can damage the health of humans, plants, and animals

B Match each sentence beginning to its ending to complete the definitions of the words in **blue** from exercise A.

1. When there is a **scarcity** of something, _c_
2. Something that is **affordable** _h_
3. If you **maximize** something, _f_
4. To **regulate** something means _i_
5. An **innovative** idea is _g_
6. If a project is **prioritized**, _d_
7. If a project is **authorized**, _e_
8. To provide **funds** to a project means _j_
9. If a building is in need of **renovation** _a_
10. To **stroll** means _b_

a. it requires repairs or improvements.
b. to walk slowly in a relaxed way.
c. there isn't enough of it.
d. it is given special importance.
e. it is given official approval.
f. you increase it as much as possible.
g. new and creative.
h. can be bought at a reasonable price.
i. to control it.
j. to give it money.

VOCABULARY SKILL Word Families: Suffixes

Knowing a word means learning its different forms, or its "family". Keep a log of different word forms. Here are examples of word families.

Noun	Verb	Adjective
creator/creation	*create*	*creative*
classification	*classify*	*classified*

Often the different forms of a word have different endings, or suffixes. Here are some common suffixes.

Noun	Verb	Adjective
-or/-er, -ity, -tion	*-ate, -ify, -ize*	*-d/-ed, -able, -ing, -ive*

C Complete the chart with the correct forms of each word. Use a dictionary to help you.

	Noun	Verb	Adjective
1.		afford	affordable
2.	authorization		
3.			innovative
4.	maximum		
5.	priority		
6.		regulate	
7.		renovate	

D Work with a partner. What other challenges do cities face? What are some solutions? Discuss your ideas. Then list them in a T-chart in your notebook.

◀ **People strolling through the High Line park in New York City, USA**

Listening A Lecture about Venice, Italy

BEFORE LISTENING

PREDICTING **A** Look at the photo. Can you guess how many tourists visit Venice each year? How do you think tourists help the city? How do they hurt it? Discuss your ideas with a partner.

WHILE LISTENING

> **LISTENING SKILL** Understanding the Introduction to a Lecture
>
> Lecture introductions often have two parts:
>
> - In the first part, the speaker provides background information about the topic or reviews what was covered in earlier lectures.
>
> - In the second part, the speaker announces the specific topic to be discussed and explains how the information will be presented.
>
> Understanding the structure of the introduction can improve your listening comprehension and help you organize your lecture notes.

B 🎧 1.3 Listen to the lecture introduction. Then answer the questions.

1. What topic did the lecturer previously speak about?
   a. how tourism has affected waterway repairs
   b. difficulties Venice faces related to flooding
   c. where Venice finds funds for large projects

2. Which *specific* topic is today's lecture going to be about?
   a. the problem of flooding
   b. the effects of the MOSE project
   c. the effects of tourism in Venice

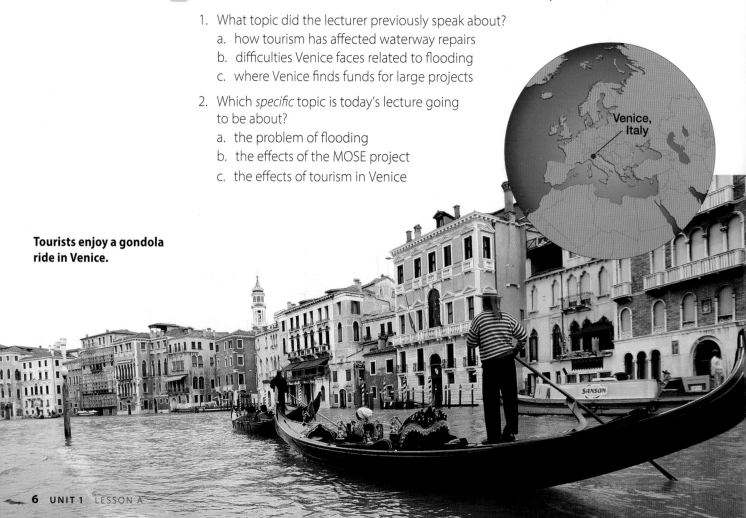

Tourists enjoy a gondola ride in Venice.

Venice, Italy

C ⌂ 1.4 ▶ 1.1 Listen to the entire lecture. Check (✓) the three main ideas.

1. _____ the impact of tourism on city services
2. _____ how tourists could change their behavior
3. _____ the causes of increased tourism in Venice
4. _____ the effects of tourism on residents of Venice
5. _____ the drawbacks of visiting Venice as a tourist
6. _____ the benefits of tourism for Venice

NOTE-TAKING SKILL Using Abbreviations

There is no right way to abbreviate words. The important thing is to remember what the abbreviation means when you review your notes. Good note takers create their own abbreviations and use them consistently. Here are some examples of abbreviations.

about/around	~	less/more than	</>	number	#	thousand	K
billion	B/bil	million	M/mil	positive	pos/+	with	w/
is/is called/ means	=	negative	neg/-	problem	prob	without	w/o

---

D ⌂ 1.5 Listen to an excerpt from the lecture. Complete the notes with abbreviations from the skill box above.

> For cent, Ven _____prob_____ of flooding
>
>   Acqua alta _____ floodwaters
>   1
>   MOSE project: > $5 _____ on H_2O barriers
>   2
> Serious prob _____ tourism
>   3
>   Tourism: _____ = profitable
>   4
>   _____ = # of tourists
>   5
> Visitors to Ven in 2014 _____ 25 _____
>   6   7
> 1 holiday wknd, 80 _____ tourists
>   8

E Work with a partner. What other forms of abbreviations do you see in the notes above? What are some examples of abbreviations you use in your notes?

AFTER LISTENING

F Discuss these questions with a partner.

1. Based on the lecture, what is the attitude of Venetian residents toward tourists? Use information from the lecture to support your answer.
2. What is the lecturer's attitude about Venice's future? Explain.

A Speaking

SPEAKING SKILL Signaling Additional Aspects of a Topic

During a presentation, speakers often use signal phrases to introduce additional aspects of a topic. This helps listeners follow along with the presentation.

Here are some common phrases you can use to introduce other aspects of a topic:

In addition, ...   Along with (previously mentioned ideas), ...

Second/Third ...   Another point I want to make is that ...

Let me add that ...

You can also transition between topics without signals.

A 🎧 1.6 Listen to an excerpt from the lecture. Complete the T-chart below.

Negative Side of Tourism	Positive Side of Tourism
Trash left behind	Generates a lot of money
_____1_____ is crowded	Tourism pays for city _____4_____
_____2_____ in parts of the economy	People have _____5_____ related to it
Serious _____3_____	

CRITICAL THINKING: APPLYING

B Work with a partner. Take turns answering the following question: What urban challenges does a city you know face? Take one minute to prepare and two minutes to present your answer. Use signal phrases to introduce additional aspects of the topic.

GRAMMAR FOR SPEAKING Passive Voice

We use the active voice to emphasize the agent, or the "doer," of an action:

In Venice, tourists **leave** a lot of trash behind.

We use the passive voice to emphasize the object of the action. It is used when the agent of an action is not known or is not important. The by phrase is often omitted.

In Venice, a lot of trash **is left** behind (by tourists).

The passive voice is possible in all verb forms (present, past, future, continuous, perfect, ...). Use the correct form of be + the past participle of the main verb.

Public parking lots filled up and **were closed**.

The problem **isn't going to be solved** soon.

More and more residents **are being forced** to leave the city.

Government funds **have been dedicated** to the project.

C Work with a partner. Look at the visuals below, and complete the conversation about the main features of the MOSE project. Use the correct form of the verb in the active or passive voice.

A: According to the photo and diagram, the MOSE flood barrier project ____consists____ (consist) of three barriers.

B: Right, and the barriers _are located_ (locate) in three places: in the Lido, Malamocco, and Chioggia inlets.

A: It looks like the barriers usually ____stay____ (stay) on the seabed.

B: Yes, they _are raised_ (raise) when high tides and storms _are forecast_ (forecast).

A: In those cases, air _is pumped_ (pump) into the hollow gates to make the barriers rise.

B: Each barrier has 78 gates, which ____move____ (move) independently of each other, so they can _be adjusted_ (adjust) as needed.

A: And when the threat of flooding is gone, the barriers _are lowered_ (lower) into the seabed.

D Work with a partner. Summarize the most important features of the MOSE flood barrier project in Venice. Include information not mentioned in the conversation above. Use the passive voice to emphasize the object of the action.

> *The gates can be raised in 30 minutes.*

E Work with a partner. Do you think the MOSE barrier will stop floods? Explain. What other defenses can cities use to prevent flooding?

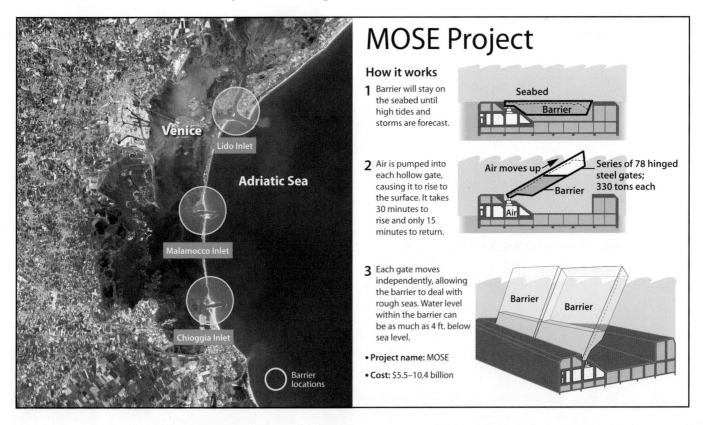

F Work in a small group. Imagine that you live by the ocean and your city was hit by a powerful hurricane. Describe the disaster using the verbs below. Use the passive voice when appropriate.

blow off	damage	destroy	flood	hit
injure	lose	rescue	trap	wash away

A: *What a terrible storm! My dog ran off, but luckily he was rescued by some neighbors. My house is OK. It wasn't damaged too much.*

B: *You're lucky! My car was hit by a tree. It's destroyed! Luckily, no one in my family was injured.*

LESSON TASK   Evaluating the Impact of Tourism

CRITICAL THINKING:
EVALUATING

A Work in a small group. Look at the list of topics. How does tourism impact these aspects of urban life? Discuss your ideas with your group. Add your own topic(s) to the list.

public transportation	job opportunities for residents
culture (arts, restaurants, and museums)	the cost of living
historical sites	the city's reputation
cleanliness	other: _____

Over two million international tourists visit Rio de Janeiro, Brazil, each year.

B Choose a tourist city that you know. What are the pros and cons of tourism there? Write your notes in the chart.

City: _____

Pros	Cons

EVERYDAY LANGUAGE   Turn Taking

Why don't I/you start?	*Who wants to go first/next?*
I'll start.	*Does anyone want to go first/next?*
I'll go first/next.	*Does anyone mind if I go first/next/last?*

C Rejoin your group. Use your chart from exercise B to tell your group about the impact of tourism on the city you chose. Explain your ideas and answer questions from the group. Use phrases for turn taking.

A: *Who wants to go first?*

B: *I'll start. I chose Muscat. Muscat is the capital of Oman. It is a beautiful city, and tourists from all over the world visit. Tourists bring lots of advantages but also some problems.*

Video

Urban Solution: Farming on Rooftops

Aerial view of rooftop garden on a parking lot in Chengdu, China

BEFORE VIEWING

> **CRITICAL THINKING** Predicting
>
> Before listening to a lecture or watching a video, look at the title and any accompanying visuals, and predict what you will learn about. Thinking about the topic in advance will make you a more active listener and increase your comprehension.

CRITICAL THINKING:
PREDICTING

A The video is about Brooklyn Grange, a company working to solve some of the problems of urban life. Look at the title and photo. Then discuss the questions with a partner.

1. What benefits do you think there are to growing vegetables on a rooftop?
2. Farming includes more than just growing vegetables. What other types of farming could be done on a rooftop?

B Match each word from the video with its meaning. Use a dictionary to help you.

1. _e_ (n) momentum   a. to do something first
2. _a_ (v) pioneer   b. main, central
3. _b_ (adj) core   c. income produced by a business or government
4. _c_ (n) revenue   d. separated, disconnected
5. _d_ (adj) alienated   e. increased speed of development or progress

WHILE VIEWING

C ▶ **1.2** Watch the video. Check (✓) the points that the speakers make.

UNDERSTANDING
MAIN IDEAS

1. ☐ Rooftop farming is having an enormous effect on cities everywhere.
2. ☐ Ben Flanner discovered his passion for farming when he came to New York City.
3. ☐ The farmers have given consideration to the soil and water.
4. ☐ Rooftop farms connect the community with the production of its food.
5. ☐ The farmers' objective is to provide most of New York City's vegetables.

D ▶ **1.2** Read the questions. Then watch the video again. Take notes as you watch. Write no more than three words or a number to answer each question.

UNDERSTANDING
DETAILS

1. Is rooftop farming practiced on a large scale or a small scale? _____

2. What type of creatures does their apiary business involve? _____

3. How long did it take to move the soil up onto the roof? _____

4. How do the stones in the soil compare to a typical rock?

   _____

5. About how much storm water a year does each farm manage?

   _____

6. What influence do the farms have on "urban heat island effect"?

   _____

E Look back at your predictions in exercise A. Were they correct? Tell a partner.

CHECKING
PREDICTIONS

AFTER VIEWING

F With your partner, discuss the questions.

PERSONALIZING

1. What experience do you have with growing vegetables or raising animals?
2. Do you feel connected to the production of your food? Explain.
3. If you were given funds to set up a farm to raise crops and animals within your city or town, where would you put it? How could you involve your community?

Vocabulary

A Match each word or phrase with its definition. Use a dictionary to help you.

1. _____ **affluent** (adj)
2. _____ **be unique to** (v phr)
3. _____ **conform** (v)
4. _____ **debatable** (adj)
5. _____ **dominant** (adj)
6. _____ **enforce** (v)
7. _____ **ethnic** (adj)
8. _____ **internalize** (v)
9. _____ **rank** (v)
10. _____ **restrict** (v)

a. relating to people with the same culture, race, and traditions
b. to occupy a position in a list or in relation to other people or things
c. to make sure that a rule is obeyed
d. to exist only in one place or situation
e. having a strong influence
f. to make a belief part of your way of thinking
g. to limit, often by official rules or laws
h. not certain; questionable
i. wealthy
j. to behave in the same way as other people

B 🎧 1.7 Complete the article with the correct form of a word from exercise A. Then listen and check your answers.

SINGAPORE

Singapore is one of Asia's most interesting countries. Among all the nations of the world, Singapore _____ only 176th in size; nevertheless, it is among the most _____, with an average income of about US$61,000. Many believe that Singapore's economic success is due to the leadership of Lee Kuan Yew, Singapore's first Prime Minister. His ideas have been _____ in Singapore for decades.

Singapore's model of success is unlike that of any other country. The model is a combination of two ideas: the encouragement of business and strict laws that regulate many aspects of life. To follow this model, the people of Singapore have learned to live and work together in an orderly way. There are laws that encourage cooperation between _____

groups, and like all laws in Singapore, they are strictly _____ by the authorities.

Things such as selling chewing gum, littering, and even spitting are all _____ by law. While these laws, some of which _____ Singapore, may surprise first-time visitors, most Singaporeans have _____ them, and for the most part, they follow the rules and laws without thinking about them.

Most Singaporeans believe that strict laws are necessary for an orderly and secure society. They are willing to _____ to the system if it makes life in Singapore more pleasant. However, for some Singaporeans and people from other countries, the issue is _____. They argue that the laws are too restrictive.

C Complete the chart with the correct form of each word. Then complete each sentence below with the correct form of one of the words. Use a dictionary to help you.

	Noun	Verb	Adjective
1.			debatable
2.		enforce	
3.			ranked
4.		restrict	

1. Dogs are _restrict_ on public beaches and in many parks.

2. The two candidates for president held a public _debathe_ .

3. In the United States, a law against chewing gum wouldn't be easy to _en force_ .

4. In the 2016 World Happiness Report, Singaporeans _rank_ 22nd in happiness.

D Read the statements about Singapore. Guess if they are true or false. Choose T for *True* or F for *False*. Then check your answers at the bottom of the page.

1. The cream-colored giant squirrel is an animal that is unique to Singapore.　　　T　　F

2. The largest ethnic group in Singapore is Malay.　　　T　　F

3. In Singapore, where you can eat ice cream is restricted by law.　　　T　　F

4. Singapore has a special government agency that enforces anticorruption laws.　　　T　　F

E Work in a small group. Discuss the questions.

PERSONALIZING

1. What is a tradition that is unique to your family? To your culture?

2. What is an important value you have internalized? Explain how it impacts you.

3. Describe a time when you chose to conform to what others were doing. Do you think you made the right choice, or did you regret it later?

ANSWERS: 1. T; 2. F (The largest ethnic group in Singapore is Chinese.); 3. F (It is not restricted.); 4. T

B Listening A Conversation about Singapore

BEFORE LISTENING

CRITICAL THINKING:
PREDICTING

A With a partner, predict the answers to these questions about Singapore.

1. What do you think Singapore is famous for?
2. Singapore is a city-state. What do you think *city-state* means?
3. Look at the photo. Why do you think the Merlion was chosen as the symbol of Singapore?

WHILE LISTENING

LISTENING FOR
MAIN IDEAS

B 🎧 **1.8** Read the statements. Then listen to the conversation about Singapore. Choose T for *True* or F for *False*.

1. The name *Singapura* means "lion city."   T   F
2. Singapore is rich in natural resources.   T   F
3. Nearly all the people of Singapore belong to one ethnic group.   T   F
4. The spirit of *kiasu* is about enjoying life every minute.   T   F
5. Nick thinks the laws of Singapore are too strict.   T   F
6. Sofia believes strict laws are a positive thing.   T   F

C Compare your answers to exercise B with a partner. Revise the false statements to make them true.

ASIA

Pacific
Ocean

Indian
Ocean

Singapore

AUSTRALIA

The Merlion, a statue that is half lion, half fish, is the symbol of Singapore.

D 🎧 1.8 Listen again. Complete the notes with no more than two words or a number.

1. Sing. started off as a _____ .

2. Modern Sing. founded in _____ .

3. Sing. is ~ _____ sq. miles.

4. Sing. = _____ % urbanized.

5. Sing. econ. ranked the _____ most innovative in the wrld.

6. Lee Kuan Yew's ideas = dominant in _____ for 50 yrs.

7. *Kiasu* = "afraid _____ ."

AFTER LISTENING

E With your partner, discuss these questions.

PERSONALIZING

1. Do you have the spirit of *kiasu*? Explain.
2. Do you think that Singapore's laws are too strict or that they're beneficial? Explain.
3. What annoying behaviors that you see in public would you like to be restricted or made illegal?

F Look at this list of regulations in Singapore and the maximum fines and penalties they carry. Take notes on what you think the purpose of each regulation is.

CRITICAL THINKING: EVALUATING

Regulations and Penalties	Purpose
1. Selling chewing gum ($100,000 or two years in prison)	
2. Spitting in public ($1,000)	_to prevent the spread of diseases_
3. Annoying people by playing a musical instrument in public ($1,000)	_to prevent people from each other_
4. Connecting to another person's Wi-Fi ($10,000 or three years in prison)	
5. Forgetting to flush a public toilet (around $150)	
6. Allowing mosquitoes to breed in your empty flower pots ($200)	
7. Feeding pigeons ($500)	

G Work in a small group. Discuss whether you think the regulations in exercise F would be a good idea where you live.

PERSONALIZING

> *I guess gum can cause problems when people don't throw it away properly. Still, I don't think I'd want it outlawed around here.*

B Speaking

PRONUNCIATION Linking with Word-Final *t*

🎧 1.9 The letter *t* at the end of a word links with the next word in these ways.

1. When *t* is followed by an unstressed word that begins with a vowel, the *t* is pronounced like a quick *d* sound.

   state of sounds like *sta dof*   *what about* sounds like *wha dabout*

2. When *t* is followed by a word that begins with a consonant (other than *t* or *d*), hold your teeth and tongue in a *t* position, but do not release air.

   right now sounds like *right now*   *street can* sounds like *street can*

3. When *t* is followed by *you* or *your*, the *t* becomes soft, like *ch*.

   what you sounds like *wha chyu*   *don't you* sounds like *don chyu*

A Look at the following pairs of words. How is the final *t* of the first word pronounced? Write the phrase in the correct column below.

1. at you	3. hit us	5. thought your	7. eight o'clock
2. upset about	4. what now	6. not you	8. not really

Like a quick *d*	No air	Soft *t*, like *ch*
upset about hit us eight o'clock	what now not really	at you thought your not you

B 🎧 1.10 Listen and check your answers to exercise A. Then listen again and repeat the phrases.

C 🎧 1.11 Listen to the conversations. Pay attention to the pronunciation of each word-final -*t*. Then take turns practicing the dialogs with a partner.

1. A: I didn't hear what you said about which plan we'll prioritize. *(ch)*
   B: I'm sorry. I'll say it again.

2. A: Do you want some tips on planning the renovation? *(No air)*
   B: Yes, I would. And how about some help with building regulations?

3. A: About that budget I submitted. Has it been authorized yet? *(No air / d / No air)*
   B: Not yet. *(d)*

4. A: What are you going to do to maximize rentals? *(d)*
   B: See that ad? We're going to put it everywhere online. *(d)*

5. A: What are you so upset about?
   B: Haven't you heard? There are no funds for that project! *(ch / No air)*

Customers play with a cat at "Café des Chats", the first cat cafe in Paris.

D Work with a partner. Read the statements related to different urban issues. Do you agree or disagree with each? Explain why to your partner.

> *I agree that smoking should be prohibited in all public places. Second-hand smoke is unhealthy.*

1. It's impossible for people from different ethnic groups to live together in peace.
2. It's the government's responsibility to provide housing for homeless people.
3. Billboards beside the road are ugly and distracting. They should be illegal.
4. In crowded cities, the government should limit the number of cars a family can have.
5. Smoking should be prohibited in all public places, both indoors and outdoors.
6. Pets should be allowed in restaurants, shops, and movie theaters.

FINAL TASK Presenting a Problem and Solutions

> You and your partner will present a problem affecting a city and propose solutions to the problem.

A Work with a partner. Discuss problems affecting a city you are both interested in. Make a list. Use your own knowledge and experience. If necessary, research the city.

PRESENTATION SKILL Presenting in Pairs

When dividing up material for a pair presentation, you can try different techniques:
- Simply divide the material to present in half.
- Take a "tag-team" approach where you take turns presenting the various points. This can help keep the audience's attention for longer presentations, but avoid switching back and forth too much.
- Assign different parts of the presentation based on who is best qualified to present each part. It's important to consider the strengths of each presenter. A qualified presenter is more confident and will make a better impression on the audience.

B With your partner, choose one of the problems you discussed in exercise A. Discuss the causes of the problem and possible solutions. Use the spider map to organize your ideas.

Causes

Problem:

_____

_____

_____

_____

Solutions

_____

_____

_____

C Decide who will present each part of the presentation. Then practice giving the presentation and make any adjustments needed.

PRESENTING **D** With your partner, present your problem and solutions to the class.

A: *We'd like to talk about the problems with the current public transportation system. This issue isn't unique to our city, but…*

B: *One place to start is to request that the city modernize the subway stations…*

E As a class, decide which pair presented the most innovative solution to an urban challenge.

REFLECTION

1. What are some useful abbreviations you can use to take notes more quickly?

_____

_____

2. What is the most useful or interesting thing you learned in this unit?

_____

_____

3. Here are the vocabulary words and phrases from the unit. Check (✓) the ones you can use.

☐ affluent	☐ enforce AWL	☐ rank
☐ affordable	☐ ethnic AWL	☐ regulate AWL
☐ authorize	☐ funds AWL	☐ renovation
☐ be unique to	☐ innovative AWL	☐ restrict AWL
☐ conform AWL	☐ internalize AWL	☐ scarcity
☐ debatable AWL	☐ maximize AWL	☐ stroll
☐ dominant AWL	☐ prioritize AWL	

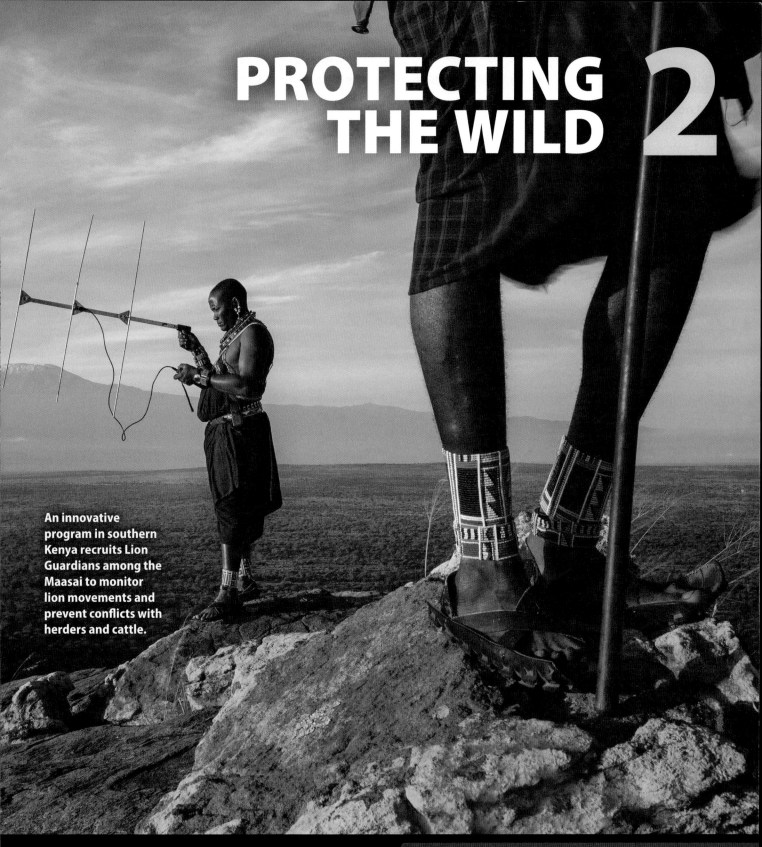

PROTECTING THE WILD 2

An innovative program in southern Kenya recruits Lion Guardians among the Maasai to monitor lion movements and prevent conflicts with herders and cattle.

ACADEMIC SKILLS

LISTENING	Activating Prior Knowledge
	Taking Notes during a Q&A
SPEAKING	Responding to an Argument
	Saying and Linking –s Endings
CRITICAL THINKING	Evaluating Arguments in a Debate

THINK AND DISCUSS

1 Where are these men, and what are they doing?
2 What are some reasons that animals become extinct?
3 Who do you think should be responsible for protecting endangered species? Governments? Companies? Citizens?

A **Look at the photo and read the caption. Then discuss the questions.**

1. Where are the man and the gorilla? What do you think the man's responsibilities are?

2. How does the photograph make you feel? Explain.

B **Read the infographic and discuss the questions.**

1. What do the 11 animals have in common?

2. What is the Photo Ark? What is its purpose?

OUR WILD FRIENDS

An orphaned mountain gorilla sits with a warden in the gorilla sanctuary of Virunga National Park in the Democratic Republic of the Congo. The orphans in the sanctuary have been the victims of poachers or animal traffickers.

MEET SOME OF THE SPECIES FACING EXTINCTION IN THE WILD

(OF THE 7,000 SPECIES IN THE PHOTO ARK)

Many species are endangered and could disappear in our lifetimes. The National Geographic Photo Ark, led by photographer Joel Sartore, is a long-term project that aims to:

- photograph every species living in the world's zoos and other protected areas
- teach and inspire the public
- help save wildlife by supporting various projects

SOUTH CHINA TIGER

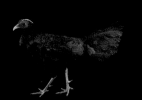

EDWARDS'S PHEASANT

SUMATRAN ORANGUTAN

MITCHELL'S LORIKEET

ARAKAN FOREST TURTLE

ATELOPUS NANAY

NORTHERN WHITE RHINO

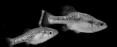

BUTTERFLY SPLITFIN

PARTULA SNAILS

RABBS' FROG (EXTINCT)

COLUMBIA BASIN PYGMY RABBIT (EXTINCT)

species

A Vocabulary

MEANING FROM
CONTEXT

A 🎧 **1.12** Read and listen to the information. Notice each word or phrase in **blue** and think about its meaning.

species?

SAVE THE WHALES!

Of the nearly 90 species of whales and dolphins, nearly all have been affected by human activity.

Are all whales endangered?

Not all, but many. The populations of most species of baleen whales[1], such as blue and humpback whales, have been significantly reduced. Their **status** today is the result of commercial whaling from the 18th to the 20th century. For hundreds of years, they've been sold for meat and oil, and some species were nearly **wiped out**. Although most whale populations have been coming back, five species of baleen whales are still endangered, and the evidence shows that many toothed whales are in danger of dying out. Hunting, **habitat** destruction, and pollution all **threaten** whale populations. In each case, humans **are to blame**.

What kinds of conservation efforts are taking place?

Many **ongoing** conservation strategies are helping whale populations. For example, the International Whaling Commission (IWC) **imposed** a ban on commercial whaling, and the United States has been leading an effort to phase out[2] whale hunting completely. Nevertheless, a number of countries continue to hunt whales.

Can whale populations recover?

Although it may be too late for some species, there are some signs that conservation efforts are working. For example, the California gray whale, which was nearly **extinct**, has made an amazing recovery and is no longer endangered.

How can you help save the whales?

You can help by learning about whales and their habitats. You can donate your time to conservation organizations. Finally, you can **modify** your behavior so that you create as little waste as possible. If we all participate in these efforts, we can help these magnificent animals **thrive**.

[1] **baleen whales** (n): whales that, instead of having teeth, have plates in their mouth that separate food from the water
[2] **phase out** (v): to bring to an end in a gradual manner

North Atlantic right whales were heavily hunted in the 18th and 19th centuries. Their name came from hunters, who said that they were the "right" whale for oil, meat, and other valuable body parts.

B Match each word or phrase with its definition.

1. __c__ are to blame (v phr)
2. _____ extinct (adj)
3. _____ habitat (n)
4. _____ imposed (v)
5. _____ modify (v)
6. __b__ ongoing (adj)
7. _____ status (n)
8. _____ threaten (v)
9. _____ thrive (v)
10. _____ wiped out (v phr)

a. are responsible for doing something wrong
b. continuing to happen
c. a state or condition at a particular time
d. the natural environment of an animal or plant
e. to grow or develop very well
f. completely eliminated or destroyed
g. to put at risk or in danger
h. no longer existing; died out
i. forced something on, such as a law or punishment
j. to change slightly

VOCABULARY SKILL Two-Part Verbs with *Out*

Two-part verbs, also called phrasal verbs, are common in speaking. Often the two words together have a new meaning. Learn them to help you speak more naturally. In two-part verbs, *out* has three basic meanings.

1. **Outside, or from inside to outside:** *eat out, take out, let out, lock out, leave out*
   Many verbs of motion can be used with *out*: *go out, run out, fly out, walk out*

2. **To distribute:** *send out, hand out, give out, pass out*

3. **To finish or end completely:** *die out, fade out, phase out, wipe out, back out, sign out, wait out*

C Choose the correct verb or verb phrase to complete the sentences.

1. One country (backed / backed out) of the whaling ban agreement at the last minute.
2. The first agreement to regulate whaling was (signed / signed out) in 1946.
3. Whales are good survivors, and very few species have actually (died / died out).
4. When the storm began, our ship headed into port to (wait it / wait it out).
5. British adventurer Tom McClean plans to (cross / cross out) the Atlantic in a whale-shaped boat.
6. A man was (handing / handing out) brochures for a whale-watching tour.
7. This copy of *Moby Dick* is missing pages. Someone (tore them / tore them out).
8. We should also protect dolphins. Let's not (leave them / leave them out).

D Work in a small group. Discuss these questions.

1. Whale-watching tours are popular around the world. Why are people fascinated by whales? If you have seen a whale, what was the experience like?
2. Should bans on hunting whales be imposed on everyone? Explain.
3. How do humans modify animal habitats in ways that can threaten the animals?
4. What are examples of "modifying behavior to create as little waste as possible"?

CRITICAL THINKING: REFLECTING

A Listening A Q&A Session about an Extinct Species

BEFORE LISTENING

PREDICTING **A** Work in a small group. Look at the photo and read the caption. Then discuss the questions.

1. What kind of habitat do you think this bird lived in?
2. The dusky seaside sparrow is now extinct. What do you think are some possible causes for its extinction?
3. What types of laws could protect endangered animals?
4. What are some drawbacks of passing laws to protect endangered species?

The dusky seaside sparrow was a bird species of southern Florida.

PREVIEWING **B** 🎧 **1.13** Listen to the first part of a question and answer (Q&A) session and look at the student notes. Notice the use of abbreviations and symbols.

> Dusky Seaside Sparrow
>
> Stat.: Extinct
>
> Former habitat: Merritt Isl., FL
>
> Causes of extinction
>
>   1. Chems used for killing mosqs.
>
>   2. Modified wetlands → no longer good habitat for sparrows

CHECKING PREDICTIONS **C** Look back at the predictions you made in exercise A. Were they correct?

WHILE LISTENING

NOTE-TAKING SKILL Taking Notes during a Q&A

When taking notes during a talk presented in a question and answer (Q&A) format, it is helpful to organize your notes according to the questions and their responses. Number the questions (Q1, Q2, etc.). Below each question, write notes on the answer, numbering (A1, A2, etc.) and indenting them as needed.

    Q1: What caused extinction?

    A1: Destruction of habitat

D 🎧 1.14 Look at the notes for the Q&A session. Notice the format. Then listen and complete the notes *only* for the questions (Q1–Q4).

Dusky Seaside Sparrow (DSS)

Q1: _____

A1: Basic cause: _____
1

DSS only on Merritt Isl. in FL. Lots of wetlands & mosquitoes

Chems used _____ mosqs. Chems killed ↑ DSS
2

Wtlnds modified. No longr _____ for DSS. Died out
3

Q2: _____

A2: Yes. Must protect animals & their _____
4

The 1973 Endangered _____ (ESA) protects both
5

Ex: steelhead trout & Columbia Riv. both protected

Q3: _____

A3: ESA diffclt to fully _____
6

Ongoing conflict betw. _____ & govt
7

Ex: gray wolf

Once common in N. Am.; 1930s—nearly wiped out

1973, wolves protected by ESA → ban on _____
8

Ranchers want right to shoot wolves that threaten their anmls

Q4: _____

A4: Situation of endangrd animals is _____ now vs. 1973
9

Now >1,400 in U.S. on endangrd list

39 spec. removed—only 14 recovrd, 9 extinct, others = mistake

Meanwhile, _____ more species to be added to list
10

E 🎧 1.14 Listen again and complete the notes for the answers (A1–A4). Write no more than two words or a number for each blank.

AFTER LISTENING

F Work with a partner. What are some reasons we should care about the extinction of species?

Speaking

> **EVERYDAY LANGUAGE**   Suggesting Ideas
>
> *I've got an idea!*   *How/What about ...?*
> *Oh—I know!*   *Did anyone say ... yet?*

BRAINSTORMING   **A** Work in a small group. Look at the list of different habitats. Brainstorm examples of plants and animals that live in each one and the dangers that they may face. Use the expressions in the skill box to suggest ideas. Complete the chart.

Habitat	Plants and Animals	Dangers
polar	polar bear	
desert		
rainforest		
ocean		

B With your group, have a discussion about the dangers you wrote in exercise A and what the animals might do when faced with such dangers.

▼ **A young polar bear leaps between ice floes in the Barents Sea, Svalbard, Norway.**

A: *Melting ice can threaten animals in a polar habitat—polar bears, for example.*
B: *I agree. I think it forces the bears to swim long distances when they hunt in the open ocean because there's no ice to rest on.*

GRAMMAR FOR SPEAKING Essential Adjective Clauses

We use adjective clauses, also called relative clauses, to give more information about a noun. The adjective clause usually comes after the noun it is modifying. An adjective clause is introduced by a relative pronoun. *Who, whom,* and *that* are used for people. *Which* and *that* are used for things. In essential adjective clauses, *that* is preferred. *Whose* is used for possessives.

Essential adjective clauses provide information that is necessary to identify a noun. The information is not optional, and commas are *not* used to separate the clause.

> *The birds **that are on the fence** are wrens.*
> *The scientist **who did the research** is available to answer questions.*

When the relative pronoun is the subject of the clause, it is followed by a <u>verb</u>.

> *We saw a sparrow **that <u>was eating</u>** crumbs on the sidewalk.*

When the relative pronoun is the object of the clause, it is followed by a <u>subject + verb</u>. The relative pronoun is optional in this case.

> *The birds **<u>(that) we see</u> in our yard a lot** are finches.*

Whose + noun is used to indicate possession.

> *The birds **whose habitat** was destroyed are at risk of extinction.*

C Work with a partner. Combine the sentences into one, adding an adjective clause after the underlined noun.

1. The police initiated an <u>investigation</u>. It led to several arrests.
2. The <u>woman</u> is an advocate for protecting wildlife. She's speaking tonight.
3. I know a <u>man</u>. He keeps two tigers as pets.
4. I think it was a <u>black bear</u>. It was to blame for all the tree damage.
5. There are many <u>people</u>. They care about endangered species.
6. The dodo was a <u>flightless bird</u>. It was wiped out in the 17th century.
7. Irresponsible <u>actions</u> should be fined. They harm wildlife.
8. Greenpeace is an environmental <u>group</u>. Its mission is to protect animal habitats.
9. The <u>wolves</u> are thriving. The government introduced them to this area.
10. The <u>tree</u> was over 200 years old. The environmentalists saved it.

D Complete these sentences with your own ideas. Use essential adjective clauses. Then share your sentences with a partner and explain your ideas.

PERSONALIZING

1. I'm fascinated by animals that _____ .
2. I really admire people who _____ .
3. Let me tell you about the time that _____ .
4. I saw a video that _____ .
5. I know someone whose _____ .
6. The teacher _____ made the students laugh.

🎧 **1.15** The letter *s* at the end of nouns, verbs, and possessives is pronounced in three ways. If you put your hand on your throat and say *zeeeee*, you should feel a vibration. This is a voiced sound. If you put your hand on your throat and say *sssss*, there is no vibration. This is a voiceless sound.

- After voiced consonants and all vowels, *s* is pronounced /z/:
  bir**ds**, mosquit**oes**, chemica**ls**

- After voiceless consonants, *s* is pronounced /s/:
  sto**ps**, resul**ts**, photogra**phs**

- After words ending in *ss*, *sh*, *ch*, *ce*, *se*, *ge*, *x*, or *z*, *s* is pronounced /əz/ or /ɪz/:
  circumstanc**es**, ranch**es**, wish**es**

When a word ending in *s* is followed by a word that starts with a vowel, the two words are linked.

      sto**ps** **a**head   *Endangered Specie**s** **A**ct*   *wish**es** **o**f ranchers*

E How is the final *s* pronounced in each word? Check (✓) the correct sound.

	/s/	/z/	/ɪz/			/s/	/z/	/ɪz/
1. hacks	☐	☐	☐	5. fifths		☐	☐	☐
2. lambs	☐	☑	☐	6. sparrows		☐	☐	☐
3. causes	☐	☐	☐	7. inboxes		☐	☐	☐
4. whales	☐	☐	☐	8. tongues		☐	☐	☐

F 🎧 **1.16** Listen and check your answers in exercise E. Then listen again and repeat the words you hear.

G 🎧 **1.17** Draw a link between the words with a final *s* and the next word with a vowel. Then, with a partner, practice saying the phrases. Listen and check your pronunciation. Then take turns making statements with the phrases.

> *Tourists in cities like to go shopping and visit museums.*

1. tourists in cities
2. animals in movies
3. causes of extinction
4. parks in cities
5. whales and dolphins
6. kids and pets *are very cute creatures*
7. images in ads
8. ponds and lakes
9. habitats in danger
10. species under protection

LESSON TASK Discussing Environmental Impact

A Read the description of the imaginary *Pristine Island*. Why do you think the land birds are decreasing? Why are the trees endangered? Tell a partner your ideas.

CRITICAL THINKING: MAKING INFERENCES

> Pristine Island is a small, undeveloped island. It has several beautiful beaches that are home to sea turtles. Wandering around the island are groups of deer, and a moderate but decreasing number of land birds live there as well. There is also a species of endangered trees scattered throughout the island.

B Work in a small group. Imagine that you are in charge of developing Pristine Island for residences and businesses, and you want to impact wildlife as little as possible. Discuss how the factors in the chart could impact wildlife. Write notes in the chart.

BRAINSTORMING

Type of Development	Impact on Wildlife
new roads	
tourists on beaches	
residential areas	
high-rise hotels	

A: *I'm concerned that animals could be hit by cars on the new roads.*
B: *That's true. The deer would probably be crossing the roads all day.*
C: *Also, when building roads, we might have to cut down some trees.*

C Work with your group. Discuss solutions to the issues you identified above. Choose three that you think could be the most effective, and share them with the class.

CRITICAL THINKING: APPLYING

> *To help minimize the impact of car accidents on deer, we will add deer-crossing signs on all major roads.*

Video

Mugger crocodiles are native to India and surrounding countries and can grow up to 16.4 feet (5 meters) in length.

Hope for the Mugger Crocodile

BEFORE VIEWING

PREDICTING **A** Look at the photo and read the caption. What do you think is the biggest problem for mugger crocodiles? Discuss your predictions with your class.

MEANING FROM CONTEXT **B** Use the context to choose the correct definition of the **bold** word or phrase in these sentences from the video.

1. Crocs live in wetlands, but most of India's swamps and riversides are now rice fields and farms. So crocs have lost **virtually** all their habitat.
   a. almost   b. not really   c. wholly   d. approximately

2. Man, this place is absolutely **teeming with** crocodiles. I just counted 140 crocodiles. Probably give or take 20 or 30.
   a. working with   b. playing with   c. filled with   d. empty of

3. But when mating season approaches, they're also intensely **territorial**, and any spot with deep water is worth fighting for.
   a. on land   b. global   c. shy   d. protective

4. Contrary to popular legend, muggers are for the most part pretty **laid-back**, sociable animals. In fact, they spend much of their time just basking in the sun.
   a. relaxed   b. happy   c. shy   d. aggressive

WHILE VIEWING

C ▶ **1.3** Watch the beginning of the video. Complete the sentences with words from the box.

UNDERSTANDING DETAILS

habitat	threaten	to blame	captive

1. Human population growth is _____ for animals' problems.

2. Growing human populations _____ crocodiles.

3. Crocodiles have lost their _____ to rice fields and farms.

4. Madras Crocodile Bank has the world's largest _____ population of muggers.

D ▶ **1.4** Watch the next section of the video. Read the statements. Choose T for *True*, F for *False*, or NG for information *Not Given*.

UNDERSTANDING DETAILS

1. The mugger has nearly been wiped out from Iran to Myanmar.   T   F   NG

2. Muggers have opportunities for success in the wild outside Sri Lanka.   T   F   NG

3. Muggers live in pools once used in agriculture.   T   F   NG

4. The muggers seem to be thriving where Whitaker visited.   T   F   NG

5. The park asked Whitaker to find out the status of the muggers.   T   F   NG

6. Whitaker thought finding one small crocodile was a bad sign.   T   F   NG

E With your partner, discuss your answers to exercise A. Were your predictions correct?

CHECKING PREDICTIONS

F ▶ **1.5** Watch the rest of the video and take notes. Then work with a partner and answer the questions.

1. What kind of conditions were the animals experiencing at the time of Whitaker's visit?
2. Why do animals coming close to the water to drink need to stay alert?
3. Why is Whitaker observing the muggers at night? What does he do as he observes them?
4. Why do the males fight? Are many of them killed?

AFTER VIEWING

G Work in a small group. Discuss the questions.

CRITICAL THINKING; EVALUATING

1. Large crocodiles can be quite dangerous to humans. Why do you think Rom Whitaker works so hard to save them?
2. What are some of the similarities and differences between the situation of these mugger crocodiles and that of the endangered species discussed in the Q&A session you heard in Lesson A?
3. After watching this video, do you think mugger crocodiles can look forward to a bright future in Sri Lanka? Why or why not?

PROTECTING THE WILD   **33**

Vocabulary

A 🎧 **1.18** Read and listen to the article. Notice each word or phrase in blue and think about its meaning.

THE YELLOWSTONE WOLF PROJECT

Wolves were once common throughout North America, but by the mid-1930s, most had been killed. In 1995, wildlife **authorities** in the United States and Canada **initiated** a program of capturing wolves in Canada and freeing them in Yellowstone National Park. This program, known as the Yellowstone Wolf Project, cost only $267,000 in government funds. It was a huge success. Today, the Yellowstone wolf population has recovered and reached a **sustainable** level.

Contrary to the wishes of many farmers and ranchers, wolf populations have also been recovering in other parts of the western United States. As the number of wolves has grown, they have become the focus of bitter **controversy**. It is **undeniable** that wolves occasionally kill sheep, cattle, and other farm animals, and farmers and ranchers naturally feel authorities are **neglecting** their rights.

On the other hand, these efficient **predators** help control populations of the animals they **prey on**, such as elk, moose, and deer. The presence of wolves also brings financial benefits to Yellowstone Park. Tens of thousands of tourists visit annually to see them. These tourists provide money for the **upkeep** of the park. Tourists also contribute about $35 million a year to the area around the park. There are strong feelings on both sides, and the Yellowstone Wolf Project will no doubt continue to be the focus of public debate for years to come.

**Wolves in Yellowstone
National Park, USA**

B Match each word or phrase with its definition.

1. _____ authorities (n)
2. _____ contrary to (adj phr)
3. _____ controversy (n)
4. _____ initiated (v)
5. _____ neglecting (v)
6. _____ predators (n)
7. _____ prey on (v phr)
8. _____ sustainable (adj)
9. _____ undeniable (adj)
10. _____ upkeep (n)

a. maintaining something in good condition _upkeep_
b. animals that kill and eat other animals _predator_
c. certain; beyond any doubt or question _undeniable_
d. able to stay at a certain level or in a certain condition _sustainable_
e. not giving something the attention it deserves _neglecting_
f. started a process or action _initiated_
g. people who have the power to make decisions and to make sure that laws are obeyed _authorities_
h. to hunt, kill, and eat (as a regular food source) _prey on_
i. serious and public disagreement _controversy_
j. different from; opposite _contrary to_

C 🎧 1.19 Read the statements. Then listen to a representative of an environmental organization calling someone to ask for a donation. Write T for *True* or F for *False*.

1. _____ The program to save great whites has been going on for a long time.
2. _____ Great white sharks don't attack humans every year.
3. _____ People think the sharks' natural behavior is to hunt humans.
4. _____ The number of great white sharks is expected to increase over time.
5. _____ Friends of Wildlife assists African officials with policy planning.
6. _____ Friends of Wildlife helps work out conflicts related to animal rights.
7. _____ Friends of Wildlife serves both animals in the wild and in zoos.
8. _____ Friends of Wildlife offers zoos financial support to maintain facilities.

D Work in a small group. Discuss the questions.

CRITICAL THINKING: REFLECTING

1. In many places in the United States, wolves are protected by the Endangered Species Act. If wolf populations have recovered, should they continue to be protected by the law? Explain.
2. If a wolf or another protected predator attacks a farmer's animals, should the farmer have the right to kill the predator? Explain.
3. Do you think the government should pay farmers or ranchers whose animals are killed by wolves or other protected predators? Explain.
4. If an organization like the Friends of Wildlife called you asking for a donation to help great white sharks, how would you react? Explain.

Listening A Debate on Legalized Hunting

BEFORE LISTENING

> **LISTENING SKILL** Activating Prior Knowledge
>
> Studies show that having some prior knowledge about a topic can improve your listening comprehension. In a classroom setting, you can activate your prior knowledge before listening by:
>
> - asking yourself or others *wh-* questions about the topic
> - discussing what you already know about the topic
> - predicting the kind of information the speaker will talk about
> - looking at any accompanying visuals such as photos, charts, or diagrams

PRIOR KNOWLEDGE   **A** Work in a small group. Discuss the questions.

1. Why do people hunt? What animals do people typically hunt?
2. Have you ever gone hunting? If so, did you like it? If not, would you try it? Explain.
3. What kinds of information do you think the speakers will discuss in the debate?

WHILE LISTENING

PREVIEWING   **B** 🎧 1.20 Listen to the introduction to a student debate about legalized hunting. Are Raoul and Yumi for or against legalized hunting? Complete the sentences.

1. _____ is arguing in favor of legalized hunting.
2. _____ is arguing against legalized hunting.

Hunters and their dogs at the Elkridge Hartford Hunt Club in Maryland, USA

C 🎧 1.21 Listen to the whole debate. Take notes on the speakers' arguments only. (You will listen for the opposing arguments in exercise D.)

NOTE TAKING

1. Yumi's 1st argument: _Hunting helps control the populations of animals such as deer._

   _____

   Raoul's opposing argument: _____

   _____

2. Yumi's 2nd argument: _____

   _____

   Raoul's opposing argument: _____

   _____

3. Raoul's 1st argument: _____

   _____

   Yumi's opposing argument: _____

   _____

4. Raoul's 2nd argument: _____

   _____

   Yumi's opposing argument: _____

   _____

D 🎧 1.21 Listen again. Now take notes on the speakers' opposing arguments.

NOTE TAKING

AFTER LISTENING

E With a partner, compare your notes above. Restate the arguments for and against hunting in your own words.

F Refer back to the debate. Which speaker presented the stronger arguments and made more effective opposing arguments? Explain your opinion to your partner.

CRITICAL THINKING:
EVALUATING

B Speaking

SPEAKING SKILL Responding to an Argument

There are specific ways to respond to an argument in a debate or conversation. First, you should acknowledge that you have heard the other speaker's argument. Then you should signal that you have a different point of view, followed by your response, or refutation.

Here are some expressions you can use to respond to an argument.

Yes, but ...	*That's a good argument, but ...*
That's possible, but ...	*That may be true, but (on the other hand) ...*
OK, but ...	*You're right that ...; however, ...*

A 🎧 **1.22** In the debate about hunting, the speakers used a number of expressions for responding to and refuting an argument. Listen and fill in the expressions you hear.

1. **Yumi:** So, for example, without hunting, deer populations would grow too large and no longer be sustainable. They'd eat all the available plants and, as a result, many animals would starve because there wouldn't be enough food for them.

   Raoul: _____ I think you're neglecting an important point.

2. **Raoul:** So, instead of allowing humans to hunt, we should allow populations of meat-eating predators to recover.

   Yumi: _____ don't forget that wolves and mountain lions don't just prey on deer and elk.

3. **Raoul:** There was also this case in Shenandoah National Park in Virginia recently where authorities caught a group of hunters who were shooting black bears and selling their body parts for use in medicines.

   Yumi: _____ those kinds of violations occur; _____ , they are rare.

RESPONDING TO AN ARGUMENT

B Read the statements below. Tell a partner whether you agree or disagree with each and why. If you disagree with your partner, use an expression from the skill box above to respond to your partner's argument with an opposing idea.

A: *I agree that humans have always been hunters. Hunting and killing animals is natural for us.*

B: *That may be true, but modern humans can satisfy their desire to hunt through sports, business, or games.*

1. Humans have always been hunters. Hunting and killing animals is natural for us.
2. We should impose a ban on fishing for a few years to allow fish populations to recover.
3. Just as humans have rights, animals have rights, too.
4. The government does not have the right to stop people from hunting on their own land.
5. It doesn't matter that the dusky seaside sparrow became extinct. It doesn't make any difference in our lives.
6. Parents should teach their children about animal rights.

C Work with a partner. Look at the chart about revenues for wildlife protection in the United States. Then answer the questions.

1. How much revenue do states bring in? How much does the federal government bring in? Is this what you would expect? Explain.

2. How much revenue is made from hunting and fishing licenses? How is it used? What is one way the money might be used to improve habitats?

3. What is the source of funds for the Federal Aid in Sport Fish and Wildlife Restoration programs? Give an example of an item that would be taxed with this type of tax.

4. At what age are waterfowl hunters required to purchase duck stamps? Do you agree with this age requirement? Explain.

5. In your own words, summarize the information this chart shows.

REVENUE FOR WILDLIFE PROTECTION

STATES

Hunting and fishing licenses — **$1.22 billion**

Helps state wildlife agencies acquire, maintain, and improve fish and wildlife habitat through the North American Wetlands Conservation Act and other programs.

Excise taxes — **$616 million**

on fishing and hunting equipment and motor-boat fuels

Helps state agencies buy land and improve fish and wildlife habitat through the Federal Aid in Sport Fish and Wildlife Restoration programs.

Licenses and excise taxes make up about **75%** of state wildlife agencies' revenue.

FEDERAL

Duck Stamps — **$24 million**

Required of waterfowl hunters age 16 and older

Purchases wetland habitat for the National Wildlife Refuge System through the Migratory Bird Conservation Fund. Sales since 1934 exceed $700 million, and 5.2 million acres have been preserved.

SOURCES: U.S. FISH AND WILDLIFE SERVICE, CHARITY NAVIGATOR

An Amur Tiger passes through the Big Cat Crossing at the Philadelphia Zoo, Pennsylvania, USA.

FINAL TASK A Debate on Wild Animals in Zoos

> You will evaluate arguments for and against keeping wild animals in zoos. Then you will organize and prepare for a debate on this issue.

CRITICAL THINKING:
EVALUATING

A Read the statements. Write F if the argument is *for* keeping animals in zoos and A if it is *against* keeping animals in zoos.

1. _____ Animals do not have rights, so it is acceptable to keep them in zoos.

2. _____ Zoos educate people about how to protect endangered species.

3. _____ In many zoos, animals are kept in small cages and cannot move around.

4. _____ It costs a lot of money to keep animals in zoos.

5. _____ It is fun to see interesting and unusual animals in zoos.

6. _____ Zoos protect animals that are hunted illegally, such as rhinos and elephants.

7. _____ People can be educated about animals without keeping them in zoos.

8. _____ The artificial environment is stressful for many animals. They often stop eating.

RESPONDING TO AN
ARGUMENT

B With a partner, take turns responding to the statements in exercise A. Use expressions for responding to an argument from the Speaking Skill box.

A: *Animals do not have rights, so it is acceptable to keep them in zoos.*
B: *Yes, but is it so clear that animals don't have rights? Some people think they do.*

C Your teacher will instruct you to prepare arguments either for or against keeping animals in zoos. Write notes to support your position. Try to predict the arguments the other speaker will make, and think about how you will respond to them.

D Your teacher will pair you with a student who prepared the opposite side of the issue. You will hold a three to five minute debate in front of the class or a small group. The student who speaks in favor of zoos should begin.

REFLECTION

1. What methods of activating prior knowledge work best for you?

_____

_____

2. Did the information you learned in this unit change your mind about protecting the wild? If so, how?

_____

_____

3. Here are the vocabulary words and phrases from the unit. Check (✔) the ones you can use.

☐ authority AWL   ☐ initiate AWL   ☐ sustainable AWL
☐ be to blame   ☐ modify AWL   ☐ threaten
☐ contrary to AWL   ☐ neglect   ☐ thrive
☐ controversy AWL   ☐ ongoing AWL   ☐ undeniable AWL
☐ extinct   ☐ predator   ☐ upkeep
☐ habitat   ☐ prey on   ☐ wipe out
☐ impose AWL   ☐ status AWL

BEAUTY AND APPEARANCE 3

A model on the runway during the Arts University Bournemouth show in London, England.

THINK AND DISCUSS

1 Look at the photo and read the caption. Why do you think people go to fashion shows?
2 How would you describe the items this man is wearing?
3 What surprises or interests you about this photo?

Look at the photo and read the information. Then discuss the questions.

1. Why do you think the man is getting a shave? Is this a common ritual in your country?

2. Do you agree with the top reasons for trying to look good? Do you think the gender differences are accurate?

3. Do you think the reasons for trying to look good change with age? With culture?

4. What other reasons are there for trying to look good?

LOOKING GOOD

How much of a person's beauty is based on physical appearance? On personality? How much depends on what a person wears? Is there a universal standard of beauty, or do these standards vary from country to country? One certainty is that looking good matters, and rituals like the one in the photo can be found everywhere.

Ali Marili gives a man a shave in his barbershop in Kilis, Turkey. Marili's father opened the shop in 1942, and his son uses the same traditional methods today.

Top three reasons for trying to look good*

To feel good about myself
60%
♂ 52%   67% ♀

To make a good impression on people I meet for the first time
44%
♂ 44%   45% ♀

To set a good example for my children
40%
♂ 39%   41% ♀

Weekly time spent on personal grooming*
4.0 h
♂ 3.2 h   4.9 h ♀

*Average across 22 countries

Vocabulary

A 🎧 1.23 Read and listen to the article. Notice each word in **blue** and think about its meaning.

HIGH-FASHION MODELING

In the world of high-fashion modeling, you don't see the variations in body type that you find with **random** people on the street. Designers have traditionally shown a **distinct** preference for tall and thin runway models to show off their latest creations. However, images of extremely thin models as seen in fashion shows and magazines can be **alarming** for some people. Some models have a height-to-weight **ratio** that is unhealthy. For example, a model might be around five feet nine inches (175 centimeters) tall but weigh only 110 pounds (50 kilograms).

The modeling business is slowly **evolving**, and the type of model that designers prefer is changing, too. The high-fashion modeling profession is no longer **exclusively** for the thinnest of the thin. The good news is that in recent years, healthy-looking models have also been seen strolling down runways. In some countries—Australia, for example—the government has even asked fashion designers and magazines to stop hiring **excessively** thin models for fashion shows and photo shoots. Now, designers **envision** people with various body types wearing their clothing. This informs their designs and is reflected in the models we are starting to see. As a result, how people **perceive** fashion models and their opinion of what **constitutes** beauty are starting to change.

A model walks down a runway at a fashion show.

B Write each word in **blue** from exercise A next to its definition.

1. _envision_ (v) to have or form a mental picture
2. _evolving_ (v) gradually changing and developing
3. _exclusivdy_ (adv) only
4. _ratio_ (n) a proportion, e.g., 2:1
5. _excessivel_ (adv) more than is necessary, normal, or desirable
6. _Constitutes_ (v) composes or forms
7. _alarming_ (adj) shocking or frightening
8. _random_ (adj) chosen without a method or plan
9. _distinct_ (adj) clear
10. _Perceive_ (v) to recognize; be aware of

C Complete the sentences with the correct form (noun, verb, adjective, or adverb) of the word in parentheses. If necessary, use a dictionary.

1. Jia was _____ when she discovered a gray hair on her head. (alarming)

2. That black hat looks _____ better on you than the blue one. (distinct)

3. The designer said the dress wasn't as stylish as what she _____ . (envision)

4. There has been an _____ of workplace fashion from formal to casual. (evolve)

5. Experts warn that the _____ use of makeup can be quite unhealthy. (excessively)

6. Members of our shopping club receive _____ discounts. (exclusively)

7. There is a general _____ that Paris is the world capital of fashion. (perceive)

8. The winners were _____ selected from the audience. (random)

D Work with a partner. Choose the word that forms a collocation with the vocabulary word in **bold** and the underlined words.

evolving

1. I never plan what I'm going to wear. I just <u>choose</u> my clothes <u>(at / for)</u> **random**.
2. <u>The</u> **ratio** <u>(for / of)</u> women <u>to</u> men in my class is 2 to 1.
3. Men's shirts <u>are</u> **distinct** <u>(to / from)</u> women's as the buttons are on opposite sides.
4. These beauty products <u>are</u> **exclusively** <u>(for / to)</u> our loyal customers.
5. The increase in extreme dieting is an **alarming** <u>(trend / movement)</u>.
6. His small business gradually **evolved** <u>(to / into)</u> a great fashion company.
7. Men who wear neckties <u>are</u> **perceived** <u>(in / as)</u> being professional.
8. Those new fashions <u>are</u> **excessively** <u>(beautiful / expensive)</u>.

E Work with a partner. Take turns using the collocations in exercise D to say sentences.

> *I don't think it's a good idea to choose your college major at random.*

F Work in a small group. Discuss the questions.

CRITICAL THINKING: REFLECTING

1. If you asked a random teenager on the street what constitutes beauty, what might he or she say? What celebrities might the teen envision?
2. If you knew someone who was excessively concerned with physical appearance, what could you say to convince him or her that attractiveness is not exclusively physical?
3. Are there any modern trends that you find alarming? Explain.
4. Society's perception of beauty always seems to be evolving, at least in certain ways. What evidence can you give of this?
5. What makes a person look distinctive?

Listening A News Report on Perceptions of Beauty

BEFORE LISTENING

CRITICAL THINKING:
EVALUATING

A With a partner, discuss the questions.

1. Look at the two rows of photos. These photos were shown to people who participated in a study on beauty. In each row, select the photo that you think shows the most beautiful face. Do you and your partner agree?
2. Look at the photos again. According to researchers, most people would choose Photo 4 and Photo 9 as the most beautiful faces. Why do you think most people chose these photos?

Row A

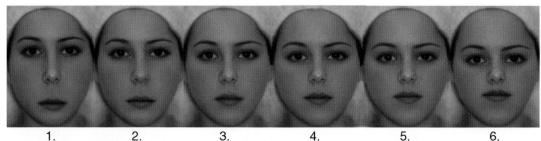

1.   2.   3.   4.   5.   6.

Row B

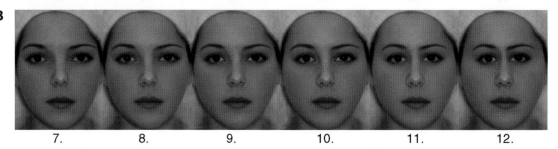

7.   8.   9.   10.   11.   12.

WHILE LISTENING

LISTENING FOR
MAIN IDEAS

B 🎧 1.24 ▶ 1.6 Listen to a news report. Match each scientist or group of scientists to their research result.

Scientists	Research Results
1. _____ Judith Langlois	a. Men's ideas about beauty and attractiveness evolved over thousands of years.
2. _____ Pamela M. Pallett/ Stephen Link/Kang Lee	b. Symmetry is a key part of what makes a face beautiful.
3. _____ Victor Johnston/David Perrett	c. There is a "golden ratio" for the ideal distance between the eyes, the mouth, and the edge of the face.
4. _____ Don Symons	d. Men prefer large eyes, full lips, and a small nose and chin.

symmetrical = متناسق يتشابه في جانبي "غالبا"

NOTE-TAKING SKILL Using an Outline

Using an outline as you listen can help you organize main ideas and details. A formal outline looks like the outline in exercise C below. Notice how the outline shows the structure of the talk, with roman numerals for main ideas, capital letters for supporting ideas, and numbers for details.

C 🎧 **1.24** Listen again and take notes to complete the outline. Write one word only in each blank.

NOTE TAKING

I. Intro: What is beauty?

    A. Does each person perceive beauty differently?

    B. Does social/cultrl _____ influence ideas?
                1

II. Studies on _____
               2

    A. Langlois

        1. ppl think _____–looking faces are beautfl
                      3

        2. symmetrical faces are beautfl

            a. far from average & symmetrical = _____ to observers
                                       4

    B. Pallett, Link & Lee—discovered "_____ ratio"
                                      5

        1. ideal dist. btwn eyes, mouth & edge of face

        2. dist. fr eyes to mouth = 36% _____ of face
                                  6

    C. Johnston & Perrett—men's prefs

        1. lg. eyes, full lips, sm. nose & _____
                                  7

        2. Symons—lg. eyes/lips = health & hlthy babies

    D. not all anthroplgsts agree about one _____ of beauty
                                            8

        1. diff cultrs have diff ideas about beauty

        2. crossed eyes, _____ & tattooed lips —all beaut.
                        9

III. Conclusion: Beauty not exclusively in eye of beholder

    A. some aspects of beauty are _____ , e.g., "gldn ratio"
                               10

    B. ppl fr. same cultr see beauty in similar ways

symmetrical

AFTER LISTENING

D Work in a small group. Discuss the questions.

PERSONALIZING

1. Do you agree or disagree that "beauty is in the eye of the beholder"? Explain.
2. Scientists believe that a beautiful face is a symmetrical face. What other features make a face beautiful to you?
3. The report said that perceptions of beauty vary from culture to culture. What are some examples of how your perception of beauty might vary from those in other cultures?

Speaking

A 🎧 **1.25** Read and listen to the article. Then look at the bar graph. What is the graph about?

THE GROWING POPULARITY OF COSMETIC SURGERY

If you think the risks of cosmetic surgery are alarming, there's good news! Cosmetic procedures are evolving; many are not excessively dangerous, and some are quite safe. You may be able to get the new look you envision with nonsurgical procedures like tissue fillers and laser treatments, which now constitute 82 percent of cosmetic procedures in the United States. Once exclusively for the rich and famous, cosmetic procedures are being chosen by more people every year.

There is a distinct difference in the way people in different cultures perceive beauty, but cosmetic surgery is a common choice in many parts of the world. The graph Top Markets for Cosmetic Procedures compares 20 countries by procedures per capita[1], total number of procedures, and the ratio of surgical to nonsurgical procedures.

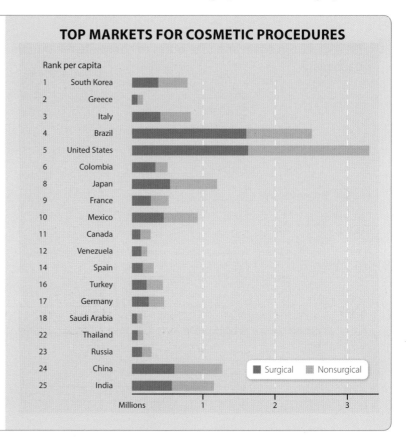

TOP MARKETS FOR COSMETIC PROCEDURES

[1] **per capita** (adj): per person relative to the total population

CRITICAL THINKING   Interpreting a Bar Graph

To understand a bar graph, it's important to study the following features:

- **the title:** tells you what the graph is about
- **labels:** tell you what the bars or numbers represent
- **the scale:** tells you the unit of measurement
- **color coding/key:** shows you what different colors mean

CRITICAL THINKING: INTERPRETING A BAR GRAPH

B Work with a partner. Answer the questions about the bar graph above.

1. What is the title of the graph?
2. Look at the labels. What do the bars represent?
3. How many countries have more than a million cosmetic procedures?
4. Look at the color coding and the key. What do the colors represent?
5. Which country has the highest number of cosmetic procedures per capita? Which has the lowest?
6. What do you find interesting or surprising about the information in the graph?

C Work with a partner. Discuss the questions.

1. Is it a positive trend that cosmetic procedures are now more affordable? Explain.
2. How has technology contributed to the evolution of cosmetic surgery?
3. Do you think the risks of cosmetic surgery are alarming? Explain.
4. What are some ways to stay young and healthy looking that avoid the need for cosmetic procedures?

SPEAKING SKILL Paraphrasing

When you paraphrase, you express something you said in a different way. Paraphrasing allows you to restate, in a clearer way, information that may be new or difficult for listeners to understand.

> *It's said that beauty lies in the eye of the beholder, yet the opposite seems to be true.* **What I mean by that is people within a culture usually have similar ideas about beauty.**

Here are some expressions you can use to paraphrase information.

I mean . . .   *Let me put it another way.*
In other words, . . .   *To put it another way, . . .*
That is (to say), . . . *What I mean by that is . . .*

D 🎧 1.26 In the news report, the speaker used a number of expressions to paraphrase. Read the sentences aloud using one of the expressions from the skill box. Then listen and write the expressions that were actually used.

1. An oft-quoted expression is, "Beauty is only skin deep." _____ , someone can be beautiful on the outside but be mean or unpleasant on the inside.

2. Another famous saying is, "Beauty is in the eye of the beholder." _____ , each person's idea of beauty is different.

3. In addition, her research shows that a beautiful face is a symmetrical face. _____ ; if both sides of the face are exactly the same, we consider a person beautiful.

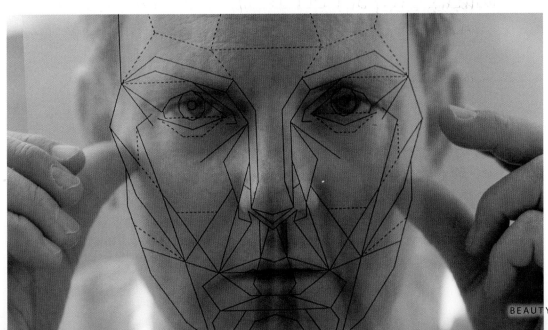

◀ **Cosmetic surgeon Dr. Marquardt uses a grid to ensure facial symmetry for his patients.**

People who smile are often perceived as more attractive.

CRITICAL THINKING: INTERPRETING

E Read these quotations about beauty. In your own words, write what each means.

1. Beauty is not in the face; beauty is a light in the heart. —Kahlil Gibran

What matters most is the beauty of a person from the inside, not the beauty of his appearance

2. It matters more what's in a woman's face than what's on it. —Claudette Colbert

what is important is the features of a woman's face, not the make-up sh wears

3. I've never seen a smiling face that was not beautiful. —Author Unknown

smiling gives our face the beauty

4. Time is a great healer but a poor beautician.[1] —Lucille S. Harper

The passage of time helps us to heal our surgeon but affects our beauty negatively

[1] **beautician (n):** a person who cuts hair and performs other beauty-related tasks for people

PARAPHRASING

F Work with a partner. Take turns reading the quotations in exercise E. Explain each quotation to your partner using a paraphrasing expression from the Speaking Skill box.

LESSON TASK Conducting a Survey

A You are going to conduct a survey about beauty and fashion. Choose four of the questions below for your survey and write two new questions of your own.

> **SURVEY QUESTIONS**
>
> - Is it better to be beautiful, intelligent, or wealthy? Why do you think so?
> - Who do you think is the most beautiful woman alive today? Who is the most handsome man alive today?
> - What is the minimum age at which people should be allowed to have cosmetic surgery?
> - What is the most unusual item of clothing you own?
> - What do you spend more money on: clothing and beauty supplies, food, or electronics?
> - Are there any fashions today that you think are strange?
> - What matters more to you is that your partner
> - is beautiful or a smart person

> **EVERYDAY LANGUAGE** Conducting a Survey
>
> When you conduct a survey, always be sure to ask politely and to thank your respondent.
>
> *Hello! Would you mind answering a few survey questions for me?*
> *Thank you. Now let's move on to the next question.*
> *That's all the questions I have for you today. Thank you for participating in the survey. I really appreciate it!*

B Interview three classmates. Ask each classmate your survey questions. Use the expressions in the Everyday Language box. Take notes on each person's answers.

A: *Is it better to be beautiful, intelligent, or wealthy? Why do you think so?*
B: *Oh, it's definitely better to be intelligent, because beauty is in the eye of the beholder, but intelligence isn't based on people's perceptions.*
A: *Interesting. Thank you. Now let's move on to the next question. . .*

C Work in a small group. Share your survey results. What is interesting or surprising about the information you heard? How would you answer each question in the survey? Discuss your thoughts with your group.

CRITICAL THINKING: APPLYING

> *The people that I surveyed think being intelligent is more important than being beautiful or wealthy. I agree with that.*

Video

Skin Mask

A model poses next to a silicone mask of her own face.

BEFORE VIEWING

A Write each word or phrase from the video next to its definition. If necessary, use a dictionary.

قالب   يبقى   كشف

| a touch of | conform | master | mold | silicone | special effects |

1. ___silicon___ (n) a rubber-like material
2. ___mold___ (n) a hollow form into which materials are put to shape objects
3. ___con form___ (v) to be similar in form, pattern, or shape
4. ___special effect___ (n) sights and sounds that seem real on TV, the radio, and in movies
5. ___a touch of___ (n phr) a small amount of something
6. ___master___ (adj) main; primary

PREDICTING **B** Look at the photo above and read the caption. This is the skin mask you will see in the video, which was modeled after a real person's face. How do you think the mold was made? Discuss with a partner.

WHILE VIEWING

UNDERSTANDING MAIN IDEAS **C** ▶ 1.7 Watch the video. Check (✓) the two procedures that are shown.

1. ☐ how the material silicone is made
2. ☐ how silicone is used to make a mold
3. ☐ how to choose a model to make a mask
4. ☐ how to make a lifelike mask from a mold
5. ☐ how a lifelike mask is used in special effects

D ▶ **1.7** Watch the video again. Put the steps for making a skin mask in the correct order from 1 to 10.

a. __1__ A cap is placed over the model's hair.

b. __7__ A master mold is prepared.

c. __3__ Artists paint her face in quick-drying silicone.

d. __10__ Makeup, eyebrows, and lashes are added to the skin mask.

e. __8__ Soft silicone is mixed with chemicals, creating a natural color.

f. __6__ The artists create a series of positive and negative masks.

g. __5__ The hardened material comes off, followed by the newly created mold.

h. __9__ The mixture is injected into the master mold.

i. __4__ The model's face is wrapped in plaster bandages.

j. __2__ Vaseline is brushed over her eyebrows and lashes.

AFTER VIEWING

E Work with a partner. Take turns reading the statements from the video. Rephrase them using paraphrasing expressions.

1. "She has to sit motionless for about an hour as the artists brush the icy cold silicone onto her face."
2. "Then the model's face is wrapped in plaster bandages, rather like a living mummy."
3. "A touch of makeup helps bring the skin to life."
4. "The completed mask has all the aspects of real human skin. It has more than just the look. It has the feel."

They choose a suitable shape for the purpose for which the mask will be made

F Work with a partner. Discuss the questions.

1. Cassandra jokes, "Who said modeling was easy?" What does she mean?
2. Explain how you think special-effects artists choose models to make their skin masks.
3. In Lesson A, you learned that standards of beauty are both universal and cultural. In Lesson B, you will learn about unusual fashions. For fashion to be unusual, it has to differ from standards. What are some fashion standards in your country that are universal? What are some that are cultural?

The positive cast on the right was made from the negative mold on the left.

B Vocabulary

[handwritten: integrates نجمع. are derived from]

MEANING FROM CONTEXT **A** 🎧 **1.27** Read and listen to a conversation. Notice each word or phrase in **blue** and think about its meaning.

Customer: Excuse me. What are these shoes made of?

Clerk: They're from an eco-fashion manufacturer that **integrates** natural materials and recycled ones. About half of their materials **are derived from** recycled plastic and metal. As it says on the label, they believe in "the **constructive** use of the waste society produces."

Customer: That's nice. But they're very unusual, aren't they? They look more like a piece of art that you would **exhibit** in a museum than shoes. I mean, they're like something an artist might **daydream** about but that nobody would ever wear in real life.

Clerk: Actually, they're very popular. I bought a pair myself, and they're **unquestionably** the most comfortable pair of shoes I've ever owned.

Customer: Really? Well, comfortable is good, but I do a lot of walking, so I'm not sure they'd be very **practical** for me. I mean, they'd probably fall apart after a week.

Clerk: Not at all. The combination of natural and recycled materials makes them **substantially** stronger than most shoes. Have a seat . . . Now, if you'll just **insert** your right foot in here . . .

Customer: Oh, this is nice! They are comfortable, aren't they? You know, I wasn't going to buy them, but you're very **persuasive**. I think I'll take a pair!

B Write each word or phrase in **blue** from exercise A next to its definition.

1. _daydream_ (v) to lose oneself in pleasant thoughts while awake
2. _integrates_ (v) combines different parts into a united whole
3. _substantially_ (adv) in a large or significant way
4. _are derived from_ (v phr) are obtained from a specified source
5. _persuasive_ (adj) able to convince people to do or believe something
6. _unquestionably_ (adv) certainly; beyond doubt
7. _insert_ (v) to put into
8. _constructive_ (adj) promoting improvement
9. _practical_ (adj) useful; capable of being used
10. _exhibit_ (v) to place on public display

C Discuss the questions with a partner.

1. Have you ever received constructive criticism? If yes, what was it?
2. What kinds of exhibitions are you most interested in?
3. What do you sometimes daydream about?
4. What is an example of a piece of clothing that is not practical?
5. What is a situation that requires you to be persuasive?

VOCABULARY SKILL Suffix –ive

The suffix –ive is added to certain verbs and nouns to make adjectives. It generally means "doing or tending to do" the action of the word it is formed from.

> persuasive = persuading, tending to persuade
> attractive = attracting, tending to attract

When adding –ive to a verb, sometimes other changes need to be made.

Example	Rule
affirm → affirm**ative**	ends in m or n: add –ative/-itive
innovate → innovat**ive**	ends in consonant + e: drop e and
define → defin**itive**	add –ive/–ative/-itive
persua**de** → persua**sive**	irregular form
repe**at** → repe**titive**	irregular form

Check a dictionary if you are not sure of the form.

D Use a word from the box and the suffix –ive to complete these opinions about fashion. Use a dictionary to help you.

| addict   alternate   construct   decorate   excess   exclude   impress   innovate |

1. I think shopping for clothes is _____—once I start, I can't stop!

2. I think it's more important to look _____ than to feel comfortable.

3. I prefer plain, dark colors and not a lot of _____ designs such as stripes, or flower and animal patterns.

4. I'm always open to criticism about the way I dress, as long as it's _____.

5. I'm into _____ fashion. I think it's boring to look like everyone else.

6. I've seen people wearing a ring on every finger, but I think that's _____.

7. That designer is _____; his clothes are really new and different.

8. Many of the stores in this area are _____; only the very wealthy shop here.

Listening A Conversation about Unusual Fashions

BEFORE LISTENING

PREDICTING **A** Look at the photos. What do you think these fashion items are? Discuss your ideas with a partner.

1. _anti gravity_

2. _____

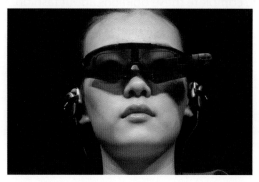

3. _____

WHILE LISTENING

LISTENING FOR
MAIN IDEAS

B 🎧 1.28 Listen to a conversation between a teenager and her parents. Look back at the photos. Next to each photo, write the name or a brief description of the item.

> **LISTENING SKILL** Listening for Specific Information
>
> Sometimes you need to listen for specific information. When you need to answer a question (during a test, for example), listening to every word can cause you to miss the information you need. Instead, underline and note the key terms related to the information you need. Then listen for those key terms and related words and phrases.

C 🎧 1.28 Read the questions. Notice the underlined key terms in question 1. For questions 2–4, work with a partner to identify and underline the key terms. Then listen again and write your answers, using the underlined terms to guide your listening.

1. <u>Where</u> was Danish clothing designer <u>Alex Soza</u> when he got the <u>idea</u> for the <u>antigravity jacket</u>? _____

2. When was Kevlar developed? _____

3. How much stronger than steel is spider silk? _____

4. Who provides funds so Ana's friend can develop wearable technology?

_____

D 🎧 1.28 Listen again and complete the outline. Write one word only in each blank. NOTE TAKING

I. Antigravity jacket

    A. part _____ , part jacket
                 1

    B. designer isn't about being _____
                                2

II. Kevlar: man-made fiber → cloth stronger than steel

    A. used to make _____-proof vests for police
                    3

    B. used to make ropes for _____
                           4

III. BioSteel: a super-strong fiber

    A. made by inserting spider-silk gene into _____
                                    5

    B. may be used to pull things up to _____
                              6

IV. Wearable electronics—integrate _____ & electrnx
                                       7

    A. Ex.: a jacket w/phone in _____
                           8

    B. Ex: GPS sneakers—to track _____ kids & hikers
                              9

AFTER LISTENING

E Work with a partner. Discuss the questions.

CRITICAL THINKING: ANALYZING

1. Can you envision any uses for an antigravity jacket, now or in the future?
2. Goats and spiders are used in the production of BioSteel. Do you think it's acceptable to use animals for the purpose of creating new textiles? Explain.
3. Are there any other uses of GPS sneakers, besides tracking lost people?
4. Do you think wearable electronics are a good idea? Why or why not?
5. Which do you think is more profitable: the fashion industry or the electronics industry? Explain.

Speaking

PRONUNCIATION Intonation for Clarification

🎧 1.29 You can ask for clarification of a term you don't know by simply restating it with a rising intonation. This invites the listener to clarify what he or she meant.

A: *That antigravity jacket was like something out of a science fiction movie.*
B: *Antigravity jacket?*
A: *Yeah. I guess you could say it's . . . it's a wearable balloon.*

A Work with a partner. Take turns making a statement about one of the devices below. Your partner uses intonation to ask for clarification and you respond.

A: *I had no idea that I walked so many miles each week until I got a Fitbit.*
B: *A Fitbit?*
A: *Yeah, a Fitbit. It's a device you wear on your wrist that keeps track of . . .*

Device	Description
Fitbit	a device worn on the wrist that counts the number of steps you take, distance walked, and calories burned
Alexa	a voice-operated personal assistant in an electronic device that can answer questions and do things for you
Ringly	a ring that buzzes when you get a notification on your smartphone from apps like UBER, Slack, Twitter, etc.
Oculus Rift	a helmet that covers your eyes and allows you to "move around" in a virtual world, usually to play 3-D computer games

GRAMMAR FOR SPEAKING Tag Questions

We use tag questions to ask if a statement is correct or if the listener agrees with us. Tag questions are formed by adding a short question (or "tag") to the end of a statement. Affirmative statements have negative tags, and negative statements have affirmative tags.

Tag questions can be confusing to answer. You should respond to the sentence before the tag.

Questions	Responses
*That doesn't sound very practical, **does it?***	No, it doesn't. [speaker agrees]
*That dog was cute, **wasn't it?***	No, it wasn't. [speaker disagrees]
*You haven't worn that before, **have you?***	Yes, I have. [speaker disagrees]
*Mom can be pretty persuasive, **can't she?***	Yes, she can. [speaker agrees]

For tag questions, use rising intonation if you aren't sure of the answer and want confirmation or clarification. Use falling intonation if you are sure about the answer and expect the speaker to agree.

B Complete the tag questions. Then ask and answer the questions with a partner, using an appropriate response and intonation. TAG QUESTIONS

1. Alex Soza is an imaginative clothing designer, _____

2. We've already discussed eco-fashion, _____

3. You'd like to learn more about fashion trends, _____

4. You're not going to wear a wool sweater today, _____

5. It's not possible to make fabric from plastic bottles, _____

6. Ana went to the fashion show with her parents, _____

7. You wouldn't wear real animal fur, _____

8. You hadn't heard about Kevlar vests before, _____

FINAL TASK A Presentation about Fashion Trends

> You will give a group presentation about fashion trends in a particular country.

A Work in a small group. First, read the questions in the chart below that will guide your presentation. Then brainstorm fashion trends in a particular city or country, and decide on the location you want to report on. Write it at the top of the chart. BRAINSTORMING

B On your own, research fashion and style trends in your location. Take notes in the chart to help you organize your ideas. Include ideas for visuals. CRITICAL THINKING: APPLYING

Location: _____	Ideas for visuals: _____, _____
What types of fabrics are popular?	
What clothing fashions are "in"?	
How do people wear their hair?	
What types of shoes do people prefer?	
What accessories do people like to wear?	
Your own question: _____	

▲ **Young men by Umeda Station in Osaka, Japan**

When preparing visuals for a presentation, high-tech options like projectors and slides are nice, but low-tech options like posters and handouts can be just as effective. Remember that the main point of visuals is to add interest and enhance your message. When preparing visuals, ask yourself:

- Is the size of the lettering large enough for everyone to see?
- Is the language clear, correct, brief, and easy to understand?
- Will everyone be able to see the photos and graphics clearly?

ORGANIZING IDEAS **C** In your group, share your notes from exercise B. Prepare a new set of notes in outline form to use during your group's presentation as well as any appropriate visuals. Decide who will present each section and which visuals they will use.

PRESENTING **D** Give your presentation. Afterwards, join with another group. Discuss each group's strengths and give any constructive feedback.

REFLECTION

1. In what situations do you need to paraphrase? What expressions can you use to paraphrase information?

_____

_____

2. What did you learn about beauty, appearance, or clothes that you will apply to your life?

_____

_____

3. Here are the vocabulary words and phrases from the unit. Check (✓) the ones you can use.

☐ alarming	☐ envision	☐ perceive AWL
☐ constitute AWL	☐ evolve AWL	☐ persuasive
☐ constructive AWL	☐ excessively	☐ practical
☐ daydream	☐ exclusively AWL	☐ random AWL
☐ be derived from AWL	☐ exhibit AWL	☐ ratio AWL
	☐ insert AWL	☐ substantially
☐ distinct AWL	☐ integrate AWL	☐ unquestionably

GOING GLOBAL 4

Visual artist Chris Milk hosts the largest collective viewing of virtual reality during his TED Talk in Vancouver, Canada, 2016.

ACADEMIC SKILLS

LISTENING Listening for Advantages

Using Columns

SPEAKING Defining Terms

Saying Parentheticals

CRITICAL THINKING Evaluating

THINK AND DISCUSS

1 What do you think these people are seeing or experiencing?

2 How do you think a virtual reality experience is different from usual viewing?

3 What would you like to view with virtual reality glasses?

EXPLORE THE THEME

Look at the photo and read the information. Then discuss the questions.

1. What type of new technology is shown in the photo? How is it useful?

2. What are some other new workplace technologies, and how are they changing the work world?

3. Look at The Future of Work 2020. Rank the drivers from strongest to weakest, in your opinion.

4. Which key skills do you think are most relevant for each driver?

Dmitry Grishin, CEO of Mail.ru, the Russian Internet giant, holding a virtual meeting with his telepresence robots

WORK SKILLS FOR THE FUTURE

The Future of Work 2020

Drivers of Change in the Workplace

| Smart machines and systems | People living longer | Big data | New media | Knowledge sharing | Globally connected world |

Key Skills Needed in the Future Workplace

2
Creative thinking

4
Social intelligence

3
Knowledge of multiple disciplines

5
Media literacy

1
Managing mental overload

Computational thinking

7
Cross-cultural under-standing

6
Virtual collaboration

A Vocabulary

pertain to

MEANING FROM CONTEXT

A 🎧 **2.2** Read and listen to the article. Notice each word or phrase in **blue** and think about its meaning.

GLOBAL EMPLOYMENT TRENDS

Globalization is producing enormous changes in **labor** markets, changes that are creating both winners and losers in the workplace. Here are two areas of change that **pertain to** both employers and employees. تتعلق

- Advanced technologies, a key **component** of globalization, are more **widespread** than ever before. New developments in technology will continue to **facilitate** tasks in business **sectors** such as architecture and engineering. It is not, however, a **promising** trend for office workers or the administrative sector, where jobs will **inevitably** be lost.

- The globalization of communication means more opportunities to learn via remote sources. Accessing information from global sources can increase a person's career **competence** and earning power. Companies who value their employees and hope to **retain**

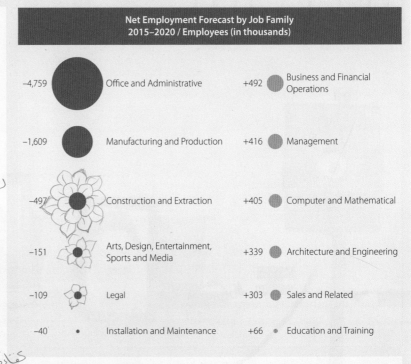

Net Employment Forecast by Job Family
2015–2020 / Employees (in thousands)

−4,759	Office and Administrative		+492	Business and Financial Operations
−1,609	Manufacturing and Production		+416	Management
−497	Construction and Extraction		+405	Computer and Mathematical
−151	Arts, Design, Entertainment, Sports and Media		+339	Architecture and Engineering
−109	Legal		+303	Sales and Related
−40	Installation and Maintenance		+66	Education and Training

them in today's competitive global environment must support and fund learning opportunities for ambitious and motivated workers—or risk losing them!

B Match each word or phrase from exercise A with its definition.

1. _f_ competence (n)   a. area of a society or economy
2. _j_ component (n)   b. to relate, belong, or apply to
3. _h_ facilitate (v)   c. showing signs of future success
4. _g_ inevitably (adv)   d. to keep
5. _e_ labor (n)   e. work or employment
6. _d_ pertain to (v phr)   f. the ability to do something well
7. _c_ promising (adj)   g. certainly, necessarily
8. _d_ retain (v)   h. to make something easier or more efficient
9. _a_ sector (n)   i. existing or happening over a large area
10. _i_ widespread (adj)   j. a part of a larger whole

C Work in a small group. Look at the information in exercise A. Discuss the questions.

1. For which sectors is the future promising? For which is globalization having a negative effect? Are any of the predictions surprising? Explain.

2. Choose four of the sectors and discuss how globalization might be expanding or shrinking the labor force in each.

pertain

VOCABULARY SKILL Using Collocations

Collocations are combinations of words that are frequently used together. Two common patterns are:

Noun + Noun (The first noun acts like an adjective.)

    labor markets   *business sector*   *earning power*

Adjective + Noun

    private sector   *advanced technologies*   *remote control*

D Complete each global career tip with the correct collocation.

1. Just knowing your _____ isn't enough these days. Learn a second one.

    a. natural language   (b.) native language   c. national language

2. Do your own Internet research to keep up with _____ in your chosen field.

    (a.) major trends   b. upper trends   c. considerable trends

3. Take a trip overseas during _____ to explore employment options.

    (a.) spring break   b. spring pause   c. spring intermission

4. Don't forget that companies often fill their _____ with local talent.

    a. superior positions   (b.) senior positions   c. elder positions

5. If you hope to work in the _____, do a leadership training program.

    a. managing sector   b. manager sector   (c.) management sector

6. If you have an _____, look for a position abroad.

    (a.) adventurous spirit   b. adventurous energy   c. adventurous body

7. Develop the ability to adapt to other cultures, as it's part of a global career _____.

    a. skill series   b. skill collection   (c.) skill set

8. Join online discussions related to your _____ of expertise or interest.

    a. specific region   (b.) specific field   c. specific environment

E Work in a group. Discuss the career tips above. Then use the collocations to make your own career tips.

> *Don't worry if you don't speak English as well as your native language. A lot of successful international businesspeople are still perfecting their English!*

Listening A Lecture about Succeeding in Business

BEFORE LISTENING

A Work in a small group. Discuss these questions.

1. What does it take to be successful in today's globalized business world?

2. You are going to hear a lecture about four skills, called "competences", needed to succeed in business today. Look at the skills and discuss what you think each means.
   - personal competence
   - social competence
   - business competence
   - cultural competence

WHILE LISTENING

LISTENING SKILL Listening for Advantages

When introducing new ideas, speakers often point out the advantages of those ideas. Listen for the following ways speakers express advantages.

- a clear statement of the advantage

   The advantage/benefit (of) ... is ...
   ... is useful/beneficial/important because ...
   ... is essential for ...

- a question before introducing an advantage

   Why is ... useful/beneficial/important?

- an explanation of what the advantage allows us to do or what it makes possible

   ... allows/helps us/you (to) ...
   ... makes it possible to ...

▼ **Doing business across different cultures requires a high level of cultural competence.**

B 🎧 2.3 ▶ 1.8 Listen to the lecture and follow along with the notes in the first column.   LISTENING FOR DETAILS

Succeeding in Business

Competences	Advantages
Personal competence	
1. understanding yourself →	helps you use time and _____ correctly 1
2. emotional intelligence →	facilitates _____ 2
3. be realistic but optimistic →	helps you be positive when things go wrong
Social competence	
1. practical trust →	helps you trust ppl to _____ done 3
2. constructive impatience →	sends message: do things _____ 4
3. connective teaching →	makes poss. for others to teach _____ 5
Business competence	
1. managing chaos →	allows you to deal w/ _____ in bus. 6
2. fluency with technology →	makes avail. latest e-bus. _____ 7
3. developing leadership →	helps bus. succeed & _____ better 8
Cultural competence	
1. understanding your culture →	allows you to value strengths & _____ 9
2. international curiosity →	allows you to look beyond yr _____ for opps. 10
3. bridge building →	allows creation of connections across cultrs

C 🎧 2.3 Listen again and complete the second column of notes in exercise B. Write no more than two words in each blank.   NOTE TAKING

AFTER LISTENING

D Work with a partner. Discuss these questions.   PERSONALIZING

1. Which of the competences that the lecturer spoke about is an area of strength for you? If possible, give an example.

2. Which of the competences would you like to develop? Explain.

A Speaking

When giving a presentation, you may sometimes use terms that are related to a specific field. Your listeners may not be familiar with these terms, and their meaning may differ from the dictionary definitions. In these cases, you should define the terms using language that your audience will understand. Here are some expressions you can use:

The term ... refers to/means ...	*By ..., I mean ...*
This means ...	*... is defined as ...*

You can also define a term by simply pausing after the term and giving a definition.

A 🎧 2.4 Work with a partner. Take turns reading the sentences aloud using expressions from the skill box. Then listen and fill in the expressions the speaker uses.

1. _____by_____ emotional intelligence, ___I mean___ understanding your own emotions and those of others.

2. ___the term___ *social competence* ___refersto___ the skills required to engage with and get the best out of other people.

3. The third component of social competence is known as *connective teaching.* ___This means___ being just as eager to learn from others as you are to pass on your knowledge to them.

4. Cultural competence ___is defined as___ an understanding of cultural differences and how to make use of that knowledge.

B Match each term related to globalization on the left with its definition on the right.

1. _b_ coca-colonization   a. the distance food is transported from producer to consumer
2. _e_ postnationalism   b. the globalization of American culture through U.S. products
3. _a_ food miles   c. inequality in access to computers and the Internet
4. _f_ worldlang   d. an active user of social media and the Internet
5. _d_ netizen   e. the process by which nations become global entities
6. _c_ digital divide   f. a new language created from several modern languages

DEFINING TERMS **C** Work with a partner. Practice saying sentences to introduce and then define the terms in exercise B. Use expressions for defining terms from the Speaking Skill box.

> *One aspect of globalization that isn't always welcome is coca-colonization. By coca-colonization, I mean the globalization of American culture through U.S. products.*

D Work in a small group. Discuss the advantages and/or disadvantages of the six aspects of globalization. Take notes below. Write an advantage and disadvantage for each.

CRITICAL THINKING: EVALUATING

Aspects of Globalization		Advantages	Disadvantages
1. coca-colonization	→	_____	_____
2. postnationalism	→	_____	_____
3. food miles	→	_____	_____
4. worldlang	→	_____	_____
5. netizen	→	_____	_____
6. digital divide	→	_____	_____

E Work with a partner. Compare the two maps. What conclusion(s) can you make about the relationship between mobile-cellular use and Internet access? Support your ideas with examples from the maps.

CRITICAL THINKING: INTERPRETING A MAP

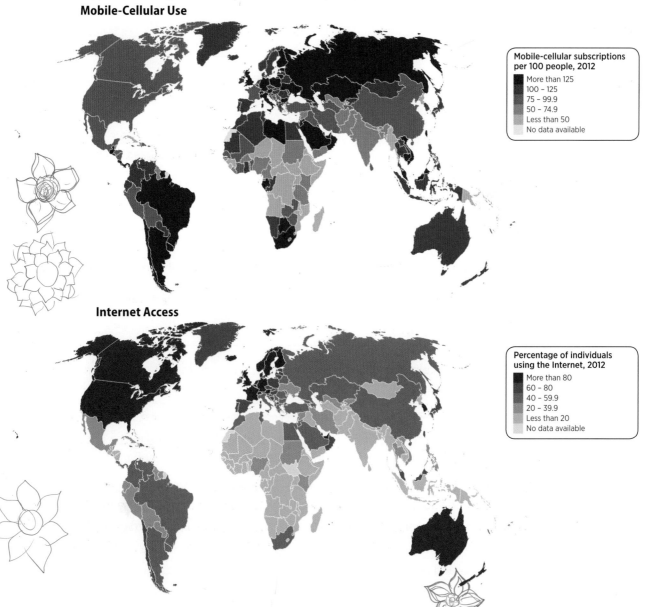

Mobile-Cellular Use

Mobile-cellular subscriptions per 100 people, 2012
- More than 125
- 100 – 125
- 75 – 99.9
- 50 – 74.9
- Less than 50
- No data available

Internet Access

Percentage of individuals using the Internet, 2012
- More than 80
- 60 – 80
- 40 – 59.9
- 20 – 39.9
- Less than 20
- No data available

GRAMMAR FOR SPEAKING Gerund Phrases

A gerund phrase is a type of noun phrase. Gerund phrases begin with a gerund (the base form of a verb plus *-ing*) and include one or more modifiers and additional objects. They are used as the subject or subject complement of a sentence, object of a verb, or object of a preposition.

> ***Being realistic but at the same time optimistic*** *allows us to stay positive—even when things go wrong.*
>
> *The first component of personal competence is* ***understanding yourself***.
>
> *You should not avoid* ***making difficult decisions***.
>
> *Social competence is essential for* ***bringing together groups of talented people***.

F Put the words and phrases in the correct order to create sentences with gerund phrases about career skills. More than one answer may be possible.

1. to think critically / is / for problem solving / being able / essential

   _____

2. are vital / accessing current information / Internet search skills / for

   _____

3. huge amounts of data / facilitate / analyzing / Big Data skills

   _____

4. a high level of / working with others successfully / emotional intelligence / requires

   _____

5. decisions / a fundamental skill / of leaders / is / making

   _____

6. many employers / is / solve problems effectively / look for / a skill / being able to

   _____

7. change / is / to welcome / a key skill / being able

   _____

8. a foreign language / toward becoming / a global citizen / is / learning / an important step

   _____

CRITICAL THINKING: RANKING

G Work in a small group. Look at the career skills. Add two more to the list. Then discuss how important they are, and number them from 1 (most useful) to 10 (least useful).

_____ a. analyzing data

_____ b. being able to think critically

_____ c. decision-making

_____ d. researching information online

_____ e. solving problems effectively

_____ f. speaking a foreign language

_____ g. welcoming change

_____ h. working with others

_____ i. _____

_____ j. _____

LESSON TASK Role-Playing a Job Interview

A Work with a partner. You are going to role-play a job interview. Look at the list of interview questions and add one more question about work experience.

> **INTERVIEW QUESTIONS**
> 1. Can you tell me a little about yourself?
> 2. What are your greatest strengths?
> 3. What is your greatest weakness?
> 4. Describe a stressful workplace situation you experienced. How did you handle it?
> 5. What is your approach to working successfully in a team?
> 6. This position requires working with people from different cultural backgrounds. What skills or qualifications do you have to work cross-culturally?
> 7. _____
>   _____

B On your own, study the interview questions and prepare your answers. Make notes to use during the interview. Use any work, school, or life experience you've had, information from this lesson, and your imagination, as necessary.

CRITICAL THINKING: APPLYING

> **EVERYDAY LANGUAGE** Asking about Experiences
>
> *Can you tell me about a time that/when you . . . ?*
> *Have you ever had the chance/opportunity to . . . ?*
> *Have you ever had any experience with . . . ?*

▼ **The Hongkong and Shanghai Banking Company (HSBC) is a globally focused company with headquarters in Hong Kong and branches throughout the world.**

C With your partner, role-play an interview between a hiring manager at an international company and an applicant. Ask the interview questions from exercise A, as well as any follow-up questions as appropriate. Use expressions from the Everyday Language box. Then switch roles and repeat.

Video

Sherpa Lives

A Sherpa replaces rope on Ama Dablam Mountain in the Himalayas.

BEFORE VIEWING

A Work in a small group. Look at the photo and discuss the questions.

1. Where do you think the Sherpa live? What might the climate be like?

2. The Sherpa people are famous for the work they do. What do you think they do?

3. In Lesson A, you learned about some of the ways globalization is affecting job markets and workers. How do you think globalization is affecting the lives and work of the Sherpa people?

WHILE VIEWING

NOTE TAKING **B** ▶ 1.9 Watch the introduction of the video, given by mountain climber and National Geographic Explorer Conrad Anker. Complete the notes. Write no more than two words or a number in each blank.

The Sherpa People

The Sherpa people → One of _____ ethnic groups w/in
Nepal [1]

Meaning of "Sherpa" → *eastern ers* [2] [3]

Activity connected to → ~~mountaind~~ *mountain climbing* [4]

Year Sherpa culture changed → _____, the year Tenzing Norgay [5]

and Sir Edmund Hillary _____ [6]

▶ 1.10 **Watch the entire video. Match each idea with the speaker who expresses it.**

1. e____ Karma Tsering
   a. Sherpa education, healthcare, and clothing have all improved.

2. c____ Conrad Anker
   b. Sherpa can earn enough money, although life feels hurried.

3. a____ Max Lowe
   c. Sherpa society has become much more connected than before.

4. b____ Kancha Sherpa
   d. Many Sherpa people are ambitious and seek success abroad.

5. d____ Mahendra Kathet
   e. Sherpas learned a modern skill thanks to a foreigner's gift.

D ▶ 1.10 **Watch the video again and choose the correct answer.**

1. Sir Edmund Hillary rewarded his Sherpa guides with watches as _____ .
   a. payment
   b. a bonus
   c. a prize

2. In terms of health care, the Sherpa now have _____ and medical clinics.
   a. an eye doctor
   b. a dentist
   c. a pharmacy

3. The only issue Kancha Sherpa is concerned about is _____ .
   a. making money
   b. dealing with tourists
   c. global warming

4. Some believe that people are losing the ability to focus on _____ .
   a. true happiness
   b. the tourist trade
   c. mountain climbing

5. An increase in food _____ has led to healthier diets.
   a. diversity
   b. production
   c. education

6. You can now use a cell phone _____ Mount Everest.
   a. at the top of
   b. from anywhere on
   c. at the base camp of

AFTER VIEWING

> **CRITICAL THINKING**   Evaluating
>
> When you evaluate, you make a judgment based on criteria. To evaluate situations or concepts, make sure you have a good understanding of the criteria you are using. This will allow you to explain your evaluation more clearly to other people. Highlight your evaluation criteria by beginning with one of these expressions:
>
> *In terms of [diet], . . .*   *With regard to [culture], . . .*   *As far as [education] goes, . . .*

E Work in a small group. Use the criteria below to evaluate this statement: *Since 1953, Sherpa life has changed for the better.*

physical well-being   technological level   traditions and culture

B Vocabulary

A 🎧 2.5 Listen and check (✓) the words you already know. Use a dictionary to help you with any new words.

[handwritten Arabic annotations throughout]

- ☑ **anticipate** (v)
- ☑ **emerging** (adj)
- ☐ **influential** (adj)
- ☐ **portable** (adj)
- ☐ **application** (n)
- ☑ **enrich** (v)
- ☐ **mass** (adj)
- ☐ **prominent** (adj)
- ☑ **collaborate** (v)
- ☑ **implication** (n)

CRITICAL THINKING:
ANALYZING

B Read the definition of *augment*. Then read the "Revealed World" section in the article below. What do you think *augmented reality* means? Discuss your ideas with a partner.

> augment (v): to make something larger, stronger, or more effective by adding to it

C 🎧 2.6 Complete the article with words from exercise A. Use the correct form of the words. Then listen and check your answers.

THE WORLD OF AUGMENTED REALITY

Augmented reality is one of the most promising and _____ global trends of recent years. This much-talked-about _____ technology is most often used to _____ the reality we see through a cell phone or other _____ device with fun or useful information, images, sounds, or videos. Some _____ of augmented reality that are already being widely used include apps that highlight and display information about restaurants, historic sites, museum exhibits, or where you parked your car. A variety of outdoor games use the technology to allow players to _____ as they hunt for digital objects. Among such games, Pokémon Go is the most _____ example; it has introduced augmented reality to a _____ audience. The augmented reality experience is also available through special eyewear or headsets, and soon even contact lenses. As we look toward the future, we _____ many more uses for this promising technology with _____ for nearly every aspect of life in the years to come.

Revealed World

Imagine bubbles floating before your eyes, filled with cool info about stuff you see on the street. Science fiction? Nope. It's augmented reality. And one day it'll be as routine as browsing the Web.

2009
Smart phone

2012
Eyewear

2020?
Contact lenses

D Complete the chart with the correct form of each word. Use a dictionary to help you.

	Noun	Verb	Adjective
1.		collaborate	
2.	implication		
3.			influential
4.		anticipate	
5.		X	prominent
6.		emerge	

E Work with a partner. Discuss these questions.

1. Look at the photo below and read the caption. What is another way that augmented reality could enrich a museum experience?

2. Would you prefer to access the Internet via glasses or a headset? Explain.

3. Do you think that augmented reality will continue to generate mass interest? What future uses for this emerging technology do you anticipate?

4. Do all uses of augmented reality enrich our lives? Or are there any negative implications of the mass use of this technology? Explain.

CRITICAL THINKING: EVALUATING

▼ **Augmented reality adds another level of information to museum exhibits. Dinosaur bones get a layer of flesh and the ability to move around at the Royal Ontario Museum, Canada.**

Listening A Podcast about Augmented Reality

BEFORE LISTENING

CRITICAL THINKING:
INTERPRETING
VISUALS

A Work with a partner. Discuss these questions.

1. Where might you see an image like the one below?
2. What kinds of information are available in the image?

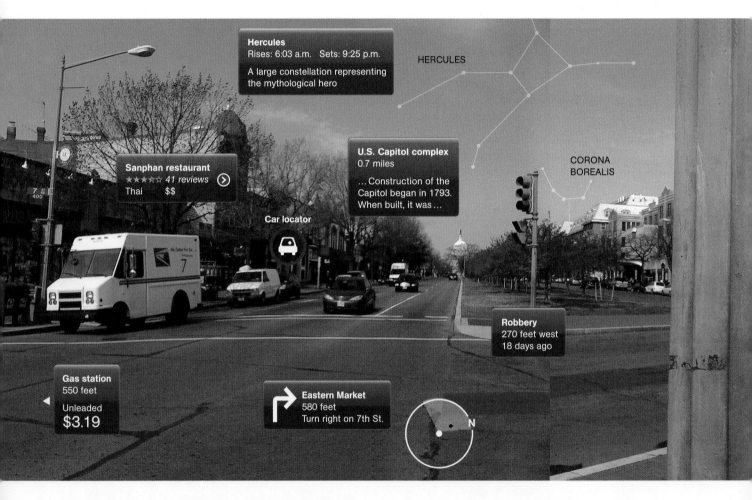

WHILE LISTENING

LISTENING FOR
MAIN IDEAS

B ∩ 2.7 Listen to a podcast about augmented reality (AR). Check (✓) the two main ideas the speakers discuss.

1. ☐ AR is a useful technology with many different applications.

2. ☐ AR's popularity has contributed to the widespread use of portable devices.

3. ☐ AR is useful when deciding which pieces of furniture to purchase.

4. ☐ AR facilitates the globalization of culture through popular games.

5. ☐ Pokémon Go's popularity has unquestionably benefited local economies.

C 🎧 **2.7** Listen again and complete the outline. Write no more than two words in each blank.

I. Intro to AR—an emerging trend in tech

   A. Combines info/images w/the _____
                                    1

   B. Later, AR will integrate sounds

II. AR has importnt implications for globalization of bus.

   A. Potential to enrich _____
                         2

   B. Could imitate facial _____ & glances
                           3

III. More ppl using AR → more affordable

   A. In industry, machines marked w/ _____
                           4

   B. Shopping for furniture—see how looks in room

IV. Pokémon GO

   A. More _____ than Facebook/Twitter in 1 yr
                      5

   B. How to play

      1. Look for animated _____ (i.e., Pokémon)
                             6

      2. Goal: capture them in your _____
                             7

   C. Reasons for success

      1. Pokémon was already a _____ brand
                           8

      2. Ppl felt better walking around outside

      3. Chances for _____ other ppl
                       9

   D. The business side

      1. Has pwr to make areas or _____
                            10

      2. Hunters may want to buy snacks, drinks, etc.

AFTER LISTENING

D Work in a small group. Discuss these questions. Use your notes from exercise C to help you.

1. What is an application of AR that would improve your own life? Explain.

2. Some believe that games that are played worldwide, such as Pokémon GO, have contributed to the globalization of culture. Others see them as global fads that have no significant impact. What is your view?

3. What are some of the benefits of the globalization of culture? What are some of the drawbacks?

Speaking

PRONUNCIATION Saying Parentheticals

🎧 2.8 We sometimes use parenthetical expressions to help clarify our ideas. We separate them with a short pause before and after. The intonation of these expressions begins a bit lower than the phrase before the interruption and rises slightly at the end. This prepares the listener for the continuation of the interrupted sentence.

Augmented reality, **or AR as it's often called***, has been a prominent trend in recent years …*
They can join meetings by phone, **which is great***, but it's not the same as being there.*

A 🎧 2.9 Underline the parenthetical expression in each sentence. Then listen and check your work. With a partner, practice saying these sentences, using correct intonation and pauses with the parentheticals.

1. That car service, though convenient and affordable, is taking jobs away from taxi drivers everywhere.

2. Pokémon GO is, at least for now, a wildly popular augmented reality game.

3. Wearable technology, despite all the advertising, hasn't had the mass appeal we'd anticipated.

4. Bollywood-style dance classes, believe it or not, are a growing trend in many places.

5. Digital art that is created for use on the Internet is sometimes, in my opinion, extremely stunning.

6. Robots and other machines, although they are undeniably useful, are causing some people to lose their jobs.

7. People born between 1982 and 2004, sometimes called "millennials," are skilled at using social media to collaborate.

8. The increase in injuries to teens, which few anticipated, is linked to the global extreme sports trend.

B Work with a partner. Make five statements about topics from popular culture (movies, TV, music, sports, fashion, technology, etc.) using the parenthetical expressions in the box below or ones of your own. Use correct intonation and pauses.

A: *Robert Downey, Jr., I think you'll agree, is a really great actor.*
B: *Oh, definitely. He was in the* Iron Man *movies, which I love, and in* Spiderman.

I think you'll agree	though I've never tried it	believe it or not
in my opinion	which I love	as far as I'm concerned

C Work in a small group. Read about four emerging global trends. Then discuss the benefits and drawbacks these trends could have on people, businesses, or organizations.

CRITICAL THINKING:
ANALYZING

A: *Synthetic food would inevitably save the lives of millions of animals.*

B: *That's true, but would it be healthy to eat? It could have some negative effects on people who eat it, couldn't it?*

1. **Synthetic food:** Plant-based meat replacements and meat grown in laboratories without harming animals will be coming to grocery stores.

2. **Virtual reality (VR):** You will be able to watch live shows and concerts and feel as if you're actually there without leaving your living room.

3. **Self-driving cars:** Companies like Tesla and Uber are creating systems that will eliminate the need for drivers and reduce the number of road accidents.

4. **Artificial art:** Computers are already writing songs and will soon be creating movies, paintings, novels, and poetry.

FINAL TASK Evaluating a Social Media Platform

> You are going to research a social media platform, evaluate its importance for globalization, and present your findings to your group.

A Work in a small group. Look at the bar graph and discuss these questions.

CRITICAL THINKING:
INTERPRETING
A GRAPH

1. How are the social media platforms ranked in the chart?

2. What do the different bar colors represent?

3. Which of the platforms have you heard of? Which have you used?

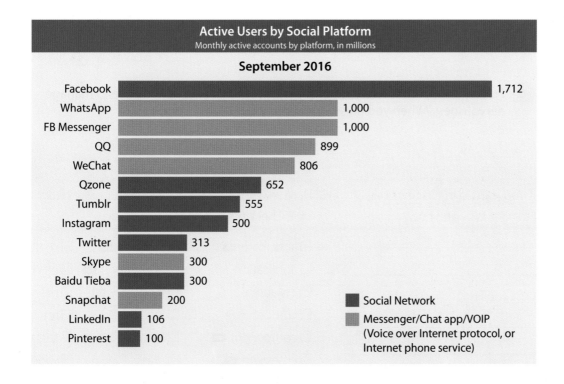

Active Users by Social Platform
Monthly active accounts by platform, in millions

September 2016

Platform	Users
Facebook	1,712
WhatsApp	1,000
FB Messenger	1,000
QQ	899
WeChat	806
Qzone	652
Tumblr	555
Instagram	500
Twitter	313
Skype	300
Baidu Tieba	300
Snapchat	200
LinkedIn	106
Pinterest	100

■ Social Network

■ Messenger/Chat app/VOIP (Voice over Internet protocol, or Internet phone service)

B Choose a platform from the graph in exercise A or another to research. Then prepare a presentation using the outline below.

I. Introduction

    A. A brief description of the platform

    B. A brief history of the platform

II. The Business Side

    A. How does it make money?

    B. Who are its competitors?

    C. How does it compare with its competitors? What are the similarities and differences?

III. Globalization

    A. Where is it most popular?

    B. How does the platform facilitate globalization?

IV. The Future

    A. Is the platform currently becoming more or less popular?

    B. How will the platform likely change in the future?

PRESENTATION SKILL Managing Nervousness

It is normal to be a little nervous at the beginning of a presentation. Because the first impression you make on your audience is important, learn to manage any nervousness. First of all, remember to breathe and be as natural as you can. Make an effort to speak slowly and calmly. Memorizing the first few sentences you plan to say can sometimes help. Soon you will feel more comfortable and confident.

PRESENTING **C** Present your platform to your group. Notice which strategy you use to manage nervousness. When you finish, answer any questions.

REFLECTION

1. What information that you learned in this unit is likely to be the most useful to you? Why and how?

_____

_____

2. What trend in the unit did you find the most interesting?

_____

_____

3. Here are the vocabulary words and phrases from the unit. Check (✓) the ones you can use.

☐ anticipate AWL	☐ facilitate AWL	☐ portable
☐ application	☐ implication AWL	☐ prominent
☐ collaborate	☐ inevitably AWL	☐ promising
☐ competence	☐ influential	☐ retain AWL
☐ component AWL	☐ labor AWL	☐ sector AWL
☐ emerging AWL	☐ mass	☐ widespread AWL
☐ enrich	☐ pertain to	

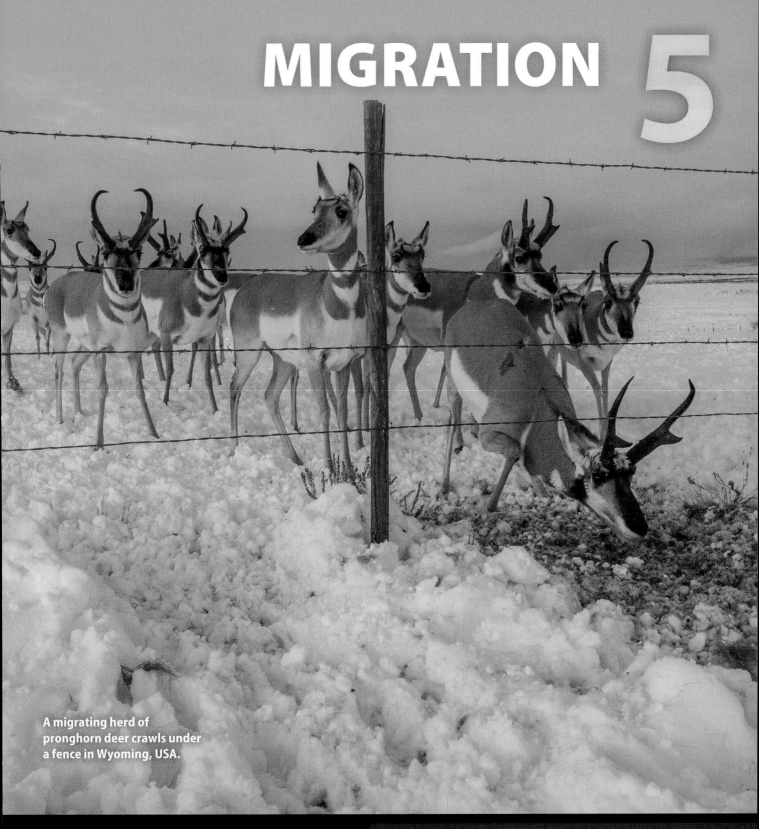

MIGRATION 5

A migrating herd of pronghorn deer crawls under a fence in Wyoming, USA.

THINK AND DISCUSS

1 Migration is when animals (or people) move from one place to another. Where do you think the deer in the photo are going?

2 What does the photo suggest about the relationship between human development and animal migration?

3 What are reasons people might move from one place to another?

EXPLORE THE THEME

Look at the map and read the information. Then discuss the questions.

1. What route is Paul Salopek taking on his journey, and how is he traveling?
2. What do you think were some reasons that early humans left Africa?
3. Why do you think Salopek is taking this journey?

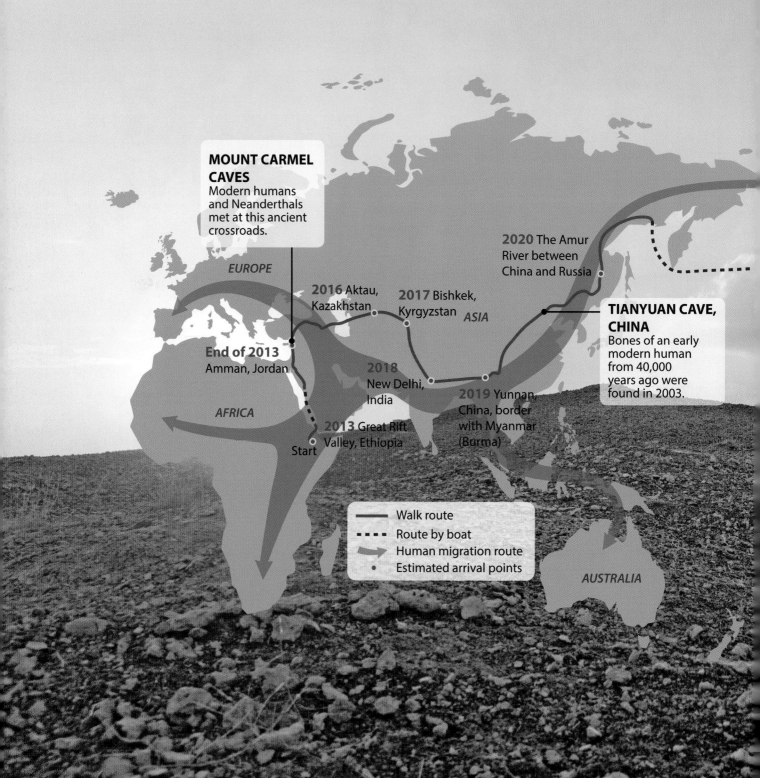

MOUNT CARMEL CAVES
Modern humans and Neanderthals met at this ancient crossroads.

EUROPE

2016 Aktau, Kazakhstan

2017 Bishkek, Kyrgyzstan

ASIA

2020 The Amur River between China and Russia

TIANYUAN CAVE, CHINA
Bones of an early modern human from 40,000 years ago were found in 2003.

End of 2013
Amman, Jordan

2018
New Delhi, India

2019 Yunnan, China, border with Myanmar (Burma)

AFRICA

2013 Great Rift Valley, Ethiopia
Start

—— Walk route
---- Route by boat
➤ Human migration route
• Estimated arrival points

AUSTRALIA

THE LONGEST WALK

Evidence suggests that *Homo sapiens* set out to discover regions of Earth some 100 to 125,000 years ago, traveling from Ethiopia's Great Rift Valley to the farthest tip of South America. To retrace their steps, writer Paul Salopek has begun his own global journey, a 21,000-mile trek that touches four continents. Calling the project the *Out of Eden Walk*, Salopek is using the latest fossil and genetic findings to plan his route. His reports from the trail are posted regularly at outofedenwalk.org.

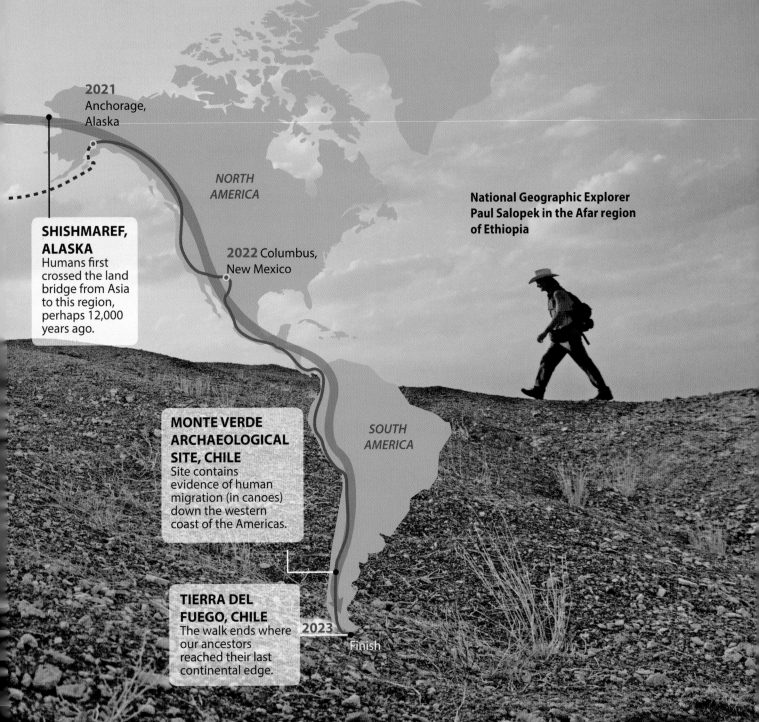

2021
Anchorage, Alaska

NORTH AMERICA

National Geographic Explorer Paul Salopek in the Afar region of Ethiopia

SHISHMAREF, ALASKA
Humans first crossed the land bridge from Asia to this region, perhaps 12,000 years ago.

2022 Columbus, New Mexico

MONTE VERDE ARCHAEOLOGICAL SITE, CHILE
Site contains evidence of human migration (in canoes) down the western coast of the Americas.

SOUTH AMERICA

TIERRA DEL FUEGO, CHILE
The walk ends where our ancestors reached their last continental edge.

2023
Finish

A Vocabulary

A 🎧 **2.10** Look at the map. Then read and listen to the information about migration. Notice each word in **blue** and think about its meaning.

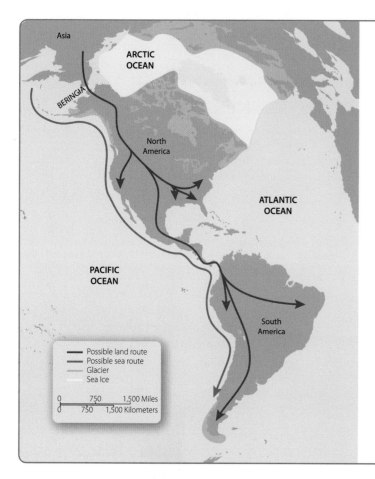

PATHS TO A NEW WORLD

No one is sure how or when the first people got to the Americas. However, recent **notable** discoveries and DNA analyses have changed our **perspective** on the first human migrations into the Americas. **Archaeologists** have found evidence suggesting that a group of perhaps fewer than 5,000 individuals **ventured** from Asia into the Americas over 15,000 years ago. This group, they believe, traveled an **immense** distance along the western coastlines of North and South America. **Subsequently**, after melting glaciers[1] had opened an interior path, a second group **migrated** from Asia following a land route. They aimed to explore and settle the central areas of the Americas. **Genetic** studies have confirmed the **hypothesis** that modern American Indians are indeed the **descendants** of people from Asia.

[1]**glacier** (n): an extremely large mass of ice

B Write each word in **blue** from exercise A next to its definition.

1. _____ (n) a possible explanation suggested by evidence

2. _____ (adv) later or afterwards

3. _____ (n) point of view

4. _____ (n) blood relatives in future generations

5. _____ (v) went into a place that might be dangerous

6. _____ (adj) extremely large or great in amount or scale

7. _____ (adj) related to characteristics of the body that are passed from generation to generation

8. _____ (n) scientists who study ancient cultures through the tools, buildings, and relics of ancient peoples

9. _____ (adj) important, interesting, or remarkable

10. _____ (v) moved from one area to another

C Work in a small group. Discuss the questions and explain your answers.

1. What is a notable discovery of the 21st century?
2. What is a good way to change a person's perspective?
3. Have you ever ventured somewhere unusual or off the beaten track? If you haven't, would you like to?
4. What can you describe as *immense*?
5. Look at the map in exercise A. On which ocean did the 5,000 people who migrated from Asia travel? About what distance did they travel in the Americas?

VOCABULARY SKILL Suffixes *–ant* and *–ist*

The suffix *–ant* is added to some verbs to mean a person who performs the action of the verb.

apply → applic**ant**   descend → descend**ant**

The suffix *–ist* is added to some verbs or nouns to refer to a person who performs an action, uses an instrument or device, or works in a certain field.

type → typ**ist**   archaeology → archaeolog**ist**

D Write a word ending in *–ant* or *–ist* that matches the definition. Use the underlined words and a dictionary to help you.

1. _____ someone who <u>participates</u> in an activity

2. _____ someone who works in the field of <u>biology</u>

3. _____ a person who studies the <u>future</u> and makes predictions

4. _____ a person who <u>migrates</u> from one place to another

5. _____ a person who draws <u>cartoons</u> for a living

6. _____ a person who <u>defends</u> himself or herself in court

7. _____ a scientist who does <u>genetic</u> research

8. _____ a person who <u>inhabits</u> a certain region

E Work in a small group. Discuss the questions.

CRITICAL THINKING: REFLECTING

1. Geneticists have discovered that information is written in our DNA. What sort of information has genetic research uncovered? What can it tell us about ourselves and our families?
2. Notable discoveries, such as the discovery of the ancient civilization of the Egyptians that thrived over 5,000 years ago, have changed the way we understand the past. Would you be interested in becoming an archaeologist and doing this kind of research? Explain.
3. A *time capsule* is a container filled with items that we hope will one day be found by others. If you were going to create a time capsule, what items would you include to best represent your culture today? Explain your choices.

Listening A Podcast about Ancient Migration

BEFORE LISTENING

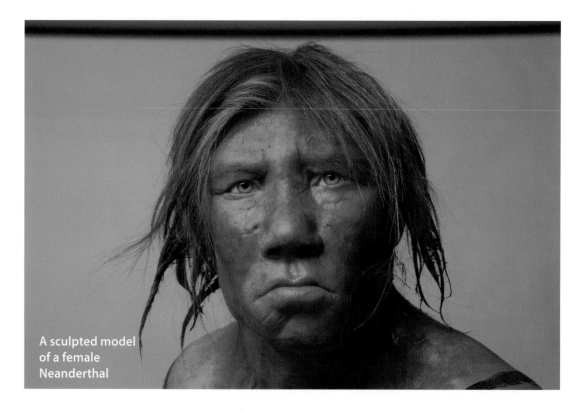

A sculpted model of a female Neanderthal

PREDICTING **A** Work with a partner. Look at the photo and caption. Then predict the answers to these questions.

1. Scientists believe that the Neanderthal were a species of ancient humans that became extinct many thousands of years ago. In which regions of the earth do you think Neanderthals lived?
2. What do you think happened when modern humans moved into an area that had already been settled by Neanderthals?
3. Do you think there is any Neanderthal DNA in modern humans?

WHILE LISTENING

CHECKING **B** 🎧 2.11 ▶ 1.11 Listen to the podcast. Were your predictions in exercise A correct?
PREDICTIONS

> **CRITICAL THINKING** Distinguishing Fact from Theory
>
> Distinguishing between fact and theory is an important skill because while facts usually remain true, theories may change. In science, facts are situations that can be observed again and again. Theories provide explanations based on facts. To distinguish between the two, it can be helpful to ask whether the information is an observation (fact) or an explanation (theory).

C 🎧 2.12 Listen to an excerpt from the podcast and write *Theory* or *Fact*.

CRITICAL THINKING: DISTINGUISHING FACT FROM THEORY

1. _____ Every once in a while, a baby is born with a slight difference in its DNA.
2. _____ All humans are related to one woman who lived about 150,000 years ago.
3. _____ Over one hundred thousand years ago, humans began migrating out of Africa.
4. _____ Scientists have found the remains of ancient humans in Australia.
5. _____ Humans were already living in Europe 30,000 years ago.
6. _____ Some Neanderthals were absorbed into the modern human family.

NOTE-TAKING SKILL Using a Time Line

When studying a topic that is organized chronologically, a time line can be the clearest and most efficient way to organize your notes. Time lines usually run from left to right, but setting up a time line diagonally or vertically can create more space for events and their descriptions.

D 🎧 2.13 Listen to an excerpt from the podcast. As you listen, complete the time line about human migration. Write no more than two words or a number.

NOTE TAKING

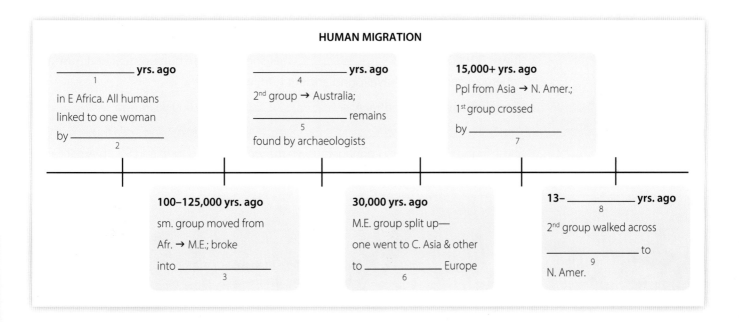

HUMAN MIGRATION

_____ yrs. ago
1
in E Africa. All humans linked to one woman by _____
2

_____ yrs. ago
4
2nd group → Australia; _____ remains
5
found by archaeologists

15,000+ yrs. ago
Ppl from Asia → N. Amer.; 1st group crossed by _____
7

100–125,000 yrs. ago
sm. group moved from Afr. → M.E.; broke into _____
3

30,000 yrs. ago
M.E. group split up— one went to C. Asia & other to _____ Europe
6

13– _____ yrs. ago
8
2nd group walked across _____ to
9
N. Amer.

AFTER LISTENING

E Work with a partner. Take turns completing the tasks.

CRITICAL THINKING: REFLECTING

1. From memory, retell the story of the journey of modern humans that you heard. If you need help, refer to the time line in exercise D.
2. The information you heard follows the story of modern humans up until about 12,000 years ago when they had reached every continent except Antarctica. There have been many other migrations of people since then. Think of an example of a migration of people in the past or present. Explain the circumstances and the reasons for it to your partner. Include any facts you know and theories you have.

A Speaking

We often need to express approximate numbers, such as amounts, dates, or times.

*I'm leaving work in **about 10 minutes**. I'll see you **around 7:00**.*

Here are some expressions you can use to mean *around* or *about*:

something like	*or thereabouts*	*-ish*	*approximately*
more or less	*roughly*	*an estimated*	*or so*

These expressions are similar in meaning to *nearly* or *equal to*:

up to	*almost*	*not quite*

And these expressions can be used to mean *not less than* or *over* (a certain value):

at least	*more than*

A 🎧 2.14 The podcast about migration included a number of expressions for approximating. With a partner, read the sentences aloud, using expressions for approximating. Then listen and write the expressions used.

1. Based on genetic evidence, scientists now think that all humans are related to one woman who lived _____ 150,000 years ago in East Africa.

2. It was 50,000 years ago _____ that some of these humans reached Australia, where archaeologists have found ancient human remains.

3. One group reached Central Asia _____ 30,000 years ago.

4. The first group crossed _____ 15,000 years ago using a sea route, keeping close to the shore as they continued down the west coast of North and South America.

Early modern humans hunt during the ice age.

B Work with a partner. Ask each other these questions. Answer using expressions for approximating.

PERSONALIZING

1. How much money would you be willing to spend on a car?
2. How much time off do you get in a year?
3. How long have you been studying English?
4. How much money do you spend per month on entertainment?
5. Think of a childhood friend. How long has it been since you last saw him or her?
6. How long has it been since you last used social media?
7. What percentage of Neanderthal DNA do you think you might have?
8. How long do you think you will be studying English?

GRAMMAR FOR SPEAKING Modals of Past Possibility

To make guesses and inferences about the past, use *could have, may (not) have,* or *might (not) have* and a past participle.

> Modern humans entering Central Asia **could have run into** Neanderthals.
> That group **might not have been** larger than a thousand people.

In short responses that are guesses, do not use the past participle.

> A: *Did they come from the Middle East?*
> B: *They* **may have**.

When *be* is the main verb, keep the past participle in the answer.

> A: *Were the Neanderthals absorbed into the modern human family?*
> B: *Scientists think some* **might have been**.

If you feel very certain something wasn't true or didn't happen, use *could not have.*

> There **couldn't have been** 10,000 people in the group that left Africa.

C Work with a partner. Read the situations and make guesses about past possibilities for each situation. Use modals of past possibility.

CRITICAL THINKING: MAKING INFERENCES

1. Samantha walked halfway to the bus stop this morning, then suddenly turned around and walked back to her house. Why did she turn around?
2. Yesterday, Ali had to go to the bank after playing basketball. Why did he go there?
3. Last week, Gabriela was offered her dream job, but she decided to turn it down. Why didn't she accept the job?
4. The lights went out in Dian's home last night. Why did they go off?
5. In the 20th century, millions of people immigrated to the United States. Why did they do this?
6. Peter got a text and then excused himself from the meeting. Why did he do this?
7. Chi failed her math test even though she had studied. Why did she fail?
8. The bookstore in our town had to close down recently. Why did it close?

D Work in a small group. Read the scenarios. Then answer the questions by making inferences using modals of past possibility.

1. Archaeologists working at a site in Oklahoma, USA, that is about 10,750 years old found evidence of early humans living there. Arrows with stone heads were found, but the nearest source of this particular stone was in Texas, at least 265 miles (426 km) away. The bones of bison, large grazing animals of North America, were also found at the site. No metal has ever been found at the site, and none was found in Oklahoma. What do these facts tell us about the early human society there?

2. It is known that Neanderthals lived in Europe and Asia when modern humans first arrived roughly 30,000 years ago. Although researchers have found a small amount of Neanderthal DNA in studies of modern humans, there isn't very much. What happened to the Neanderthals, and why?

E With your group, look at the photo. Use past modals to make inferences about who drew them, how they were drawn, how humans lived at that time, why they made these drawings, and so on.

A: *The pictures of animals may have been drawn by the first modern humans.*

B: *No, they couldn't have been. Modern humans hadn't arrived in Europe yet.*

C: *Neanderthals at that time might have been more skilled at drawing than modern humans.*

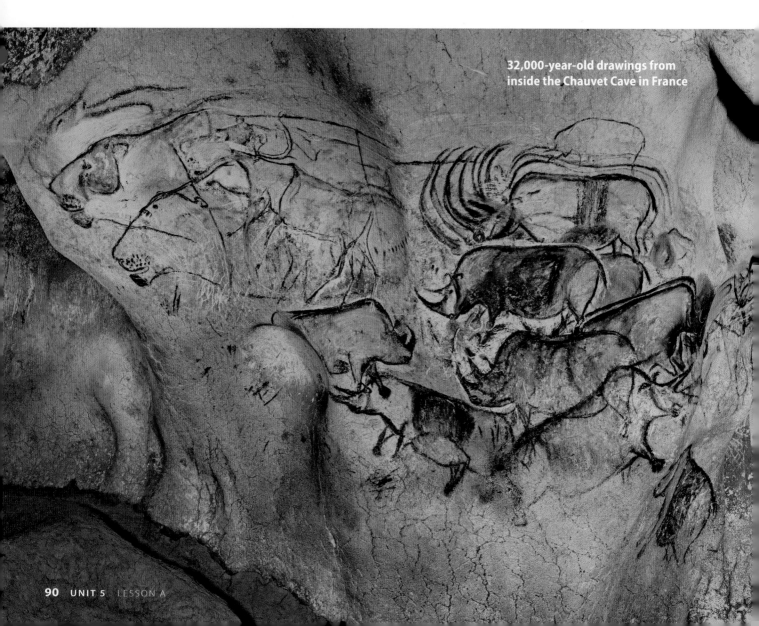

32,000-year-old drawings from inside the Chauvet Cave in France

LESSON TASK Discussing Family Origins

A Where did your family members come from originally? If they left that place, where did they go? Complete the chart with information about your family. If you are not sure about something, write a question mark.

ORGANIZING IDEAS

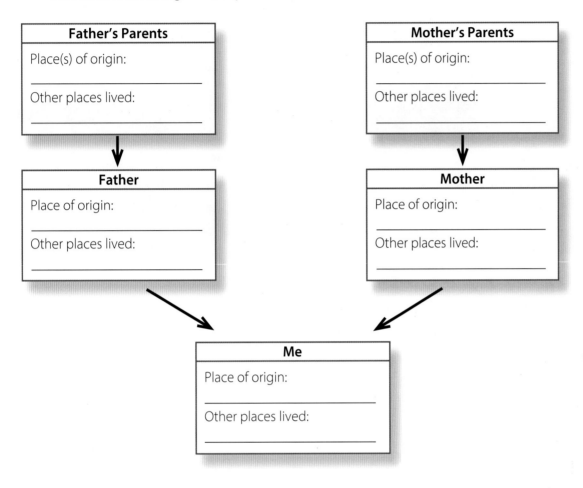

Father's Parents
Place(s) of origin:
_____
Other places lived:
_____

Mother's Parents
Place(s) of origin:
_____
Other places lived:
_____

Father
Place of origin:
_____
Other places lived:
_____

Mother
Place of origin:
_____
Other places lived:
_____

Me
Place of origin:
_____
Other places lived:
_____

EVERYDAY LANGUAGE Showing Surprise

Informal:	*You're kidding (me).*	*That's incredible.*
	Are you serious?	*No way.*
Formal:	*That's really (quite) surprising.*	*That's hard to believe.*
	I never would have guessed.	*I was surprised to learn that… .*

B Work in a small group. Use the information from exercise A to talk about your family. Say where your family members are from and where they have lived. If you are not sure, make a guess. Use expressions of surprise where appropriate.

A: *I was born in Chicago, and my parents were born in Holland. They came to the U.S. in 1967 or so. I'm not sure about my mother's parents. I think they may have migrated from Poland.*

B: *You're kidding. That's where my grandmother is from.*

Video

Wildebeest, zebra, and European storks in Serengeti National Park, Tanzania

Wildebeest Migration

KENYA

TANZANIA

Ikorongo Game Reserve

Grumeti Game Reserve

Loliondo Game Controlled Area

Maswa Game Reserve

NCAA

Ndutu

Serengeti National Park Migration:
1. Jan-Feb-Mar-April
2. May
3. June-July
4. Aug-Sep
5. Oct
6. Nov-Dec

BEFORE VIEWING

CRITICAL THINKING: INTERPRETING A MAP

A Look at the map and answer the questions.

1. Which two countries does the wildebeest migration travel through?

_____   _____

2. Use the key to follow the migration of the wildebeest throughout the year. Where are the wildebeest today?

_____

B Match each word in **bold** from the video with its definition.

1. _____ the **calves** can run
2. _____ **carcasses** are left behind
3. _____ wildebeest **grazed** these plains
4. _____ the migrating **herds** arrive
5. _____ **sniff** the air
6. _____ what **triggers** the migration

a. ate grass or other growing plants
b. large groups of animals of one kind
c. young wildebeest
d. the bodies of a dead animals
e. causes an event to happen
f. to smell

WHILE VIEWING

C ▶ **1.12** Watch the video. Does the speaker make these points? Check (✓) the correct answer(s).

UNDERSTANDING
MAIN IDEAS

	Yes	No
1. The wildebeest make a massive round-trip journey each year.	☐	☐
2. The migration begins when the herd leader sniffs the air.	☐	☐
3. Not all the animals that begin the migration will make it back.	☐	☐
4. Harsh weather conditions are the main threat to the wildebeest.	☐	☐
5. The journey back begins right after the animals have given birth.	☐	☐

D ▶ **1.12** Watch the video again. Complete the notes. Write no more than three words or a number for each.

NOTE TAKING

<u>Wildebeest Migration</u>

- 2 mil. animals travel almost _____1_____ miles
- Wildebeest grazed plains more than _____2_____ yrs. ago
- At beg. of yr., all wldbst give _____3_____ in same mo.
  - Calves can run _____4_____ their mothers w/in 2 days
- Nobody knows what _____5_____
- ~200K of _____6_____ wldbst die of starvation, disease, exhaustion
  - Others die from preds.; cat tries to separate calf from _____7_____
- Kenya's Maasai Mara: _____8_____ create huge area of watered _____9_____
- In Nov., wldbst head south again to the _____10_____

AFTER VIEWING

E Work with a partner. Discuss the questions.

CRITICAL THINKING:
EVALUATING

1. In the video, you heard that "no one knows what triggers the migration." What are some possible explanations for why the wildebeest start their migration?
2. Recently, the government of Tanzania wanted to build a highway across the Serengeti National Park. The road would have cut across the migration routes of the wildebeest. What arguments could be made against building this highway? What arguments could be made in favor of building it?
3. How do you think human and animal migrations are similar? How are they different?
4. Every year a great animal migration in Tanzania attracts nearly 200,000 tourists to the area. Would you also call this movement of humans a migration? Explain.

A 🎧 **2.15** Look at the map and the map key of the Greater Yellowstone Ecosystem. Then read and listen to the description. Notice each word or phrase in blue and think about its meaning.

THE GREATER YELLOWSTONE ECOSYSTEM

Yellowstone National Park is a nearly 35,000-square-mile wilderness recreation area in western United States. Yellowstone features canyons, rivers, forests, hot springs, and geysers. It is home to hundreds of animal species, including bears, wolves, bison, elk, and antelope.

Wildlife within Yellowstone National Park itself is protected by **legislation**, but the **ecology** of the park—the plants and animals— extends beyond its borders, where the area is divided among federal, state, private, and **tribal** lands. Conflicting interests create nearly **overwhelming** challenges that conservation managers must **confront** as they **monitor** animal movement in and around the park.

On privately owned land, wildlife habitat is **diminishing**. Development often **interferes** with animal migration, and ancient migration routes are being **displaced**. However, some private land is being protected. Billionaire[1] Ted Turner is **dedicated to** helping wildlife; his Flying D Ranch protects some 113,000 acres of wildlife habitat.

Landownership

- National Park Service
- Wilderness
- U.S. Forest Service
- Private Protected
- Fish and Wildlife Service
- Bureau of Land Management
- Tribal
- State and Local Government
- Private
- Other

Madison Valley Elk Herd

- Summer Range
- Winter Range
- — Migration Route

Lines represent seasonal migrations between summer and winter ranges for 11 elk in the Madison Valley herd. GPS collars collected data on their locations every 30 minutes.

[1]**billionaire** (n): a person with more than one billion (1,000,000,000) dollars

B Match each word or phrase with its definition.

1. _____ confront (v)
2. _____ dedicated to (adj)
3. _____ diminish (v)
4. _____ displace (v)
5. _____ ecology (n)
6. _____ interfere (v)
7. _____ legislation (n)
8. _____ monitor (v)
9. _____ overwhelming (adj)
10. _____ tribal (adj)

a. a habitat, its living things, and their relationships
b. to deal with or face (a problem or challenge)
c. more than can be managed or dealt with
d. to block or get in the way of an activity or goal
e. to follow, check, or observe
f. to get smaller in size, number, importance, etc.
g. belonging or related to a group of native people
h. to force to move from a home or habitat
i. a law or laws
j. very involved in and supportive of

C Work with a partner. Look at the map in exercise A and answer the questions.

1. How was information about the movements of elk obtained?
2. Do the elk spend the winter inside or outside Yellowstone National Park?
3. Do any elk migration routes go through the Flying D Ranch?
4. Who owns the land between Big Sky and the Big Sky Resort?
5. Is there any private protected land in Madison Valley?

CRITICAL THINKING:
INTERPRETING A MAP

D Work in a small group. Read these statements by people living in the Greater Yellowstone Ecosystem. Which landownership group(s) on the map in exercise A might each person belong to?

CRITICAL THINKING:
EVALUATING

1. It is of the greatest importance to protect the ecology of the area and live in harmony with nature here as our ancestors did.
2. We need stricter legislation to keep people from interfering with living things in the rivers, streams, and forests.
3. If I don't displace animals from time to time, I won't be able to develop my land. This isn't state land, after all. It's my property.
4. We're dedicated to confronting the problem of diminishing predator populations and believe introducing more bears and wolves into the area is a great solution.
5. A herd of migrating elk can be overwhelming for a town. It's my job to see that they get the resources they need to deal with it.

▸ **Herd of elk in summer in Yellowstone, USA**

Listening A Conversation about the Serengeti

BEFORE LISTENING

A Work in a small group. Discuss the questions.

1. What have you learned about the Serengeti National Park in Tanzania and Kenya? Discuss what makes the Serengeti interesting and a popular tourist destination.
2. Think about Yellowstone National Park and the conservation challenges it faces. Could the Serengeti National Park in Tanzania face similar challenges? Explain.

WHILE LISTENING

B 🎧 2.16 Listen to the conversation. Choose the correct answers.

1. The size of the Serengeti Mara ecosystem has (increased / diminished).
2. The human populations in Kenya and Tanzania have been (increasing / decreasing).
3. Offers of money from tourism companies (have / haven't) persuaded the Robandans to move from their village.
4. Animal populations in the Serengeti Mara ecosystem are (at risk / maintaining their numbers).

C 🎧 2.16 Listen again. Choose T for *True*, F for *False*, or NG for information *Not Given*.

1. In 1950, the authorities felt the animals were a higher priority than the Ikoma people. T F NG

2. Everyone who eats bush meat in Tanzania is punished for it. T F NG

3. An ecotourism group has invested a lot of money to protect the ecology of the Serengeti. T F NG

4. The tourism companies are planning to force the Robandans to move. T F NG

5. Brandon suggests that the tourism companies are only concerned with money. T F NG

6. Ashley is going to go on a trip soon. T F NG

LISTENING SKILL Listening for Clarification

In conversation, speakers often clarify what they have said so that their intended meaning is clear.

Some expressions that signal clarification are:

> *For the most part yes, although...*   *Well, yes/yeah,..., but...*
> *Yes/Yeah, partly. But...*   *Well, you're right that..., but...*
> *That's true, but...*   *Of course, but...*

If you listen for what comes after these expressions, you will better understand the speaker's meaning.

D Read these sentences expressing what Ashley thought before Brandon added a clarification. Then listen to excerpts from their discussion and write the clarification that Brandon provided.

1. Brandon spent his vacation in Tanzania.

   _____

2. The wildebeest migration takes place in the Serengeti National Park.

   _____

3. 16,700 square kilometers is a huge amount of land to set aside for wildlife.

   _____

4. Hunting, selling, and eating bush meat must be under control because it's illegal.

   _____

5. The ecotourism company Brandon mentions is only interested in making money.

   _____

AFTER LISTENING

E Discuss the questions with a partner.

1. In your own words, how would you explain the conflict between the needs of the animals and the needs of people of the Serengeti Mara ecosystem?
2. If you were villagers from Robanda, would you accept the offer of money to move off the land? What would you gain, and what would you lose from your decision?
3. What if, instead of persuading the Ikoma to leave, the tourism companies invited them to be partners in the business? How would the two groups cooperate to give visitors a great experience of the Serengeti? What difficulties might interfere with this collaboration?

Lions in Serengeti National Park, Tanzania

B Speaking

PRONUNCIATION Linking with *You* or *Your*

🎧 **2.18** We often link a word that ends in the sound /t/, /d/, or /z/ with *you* or *your*. Those sounds are softened and change as follows:

- /t/ sounds like /tʃ/   *I see what you mean.*
- /d/ sounds like /dʒ/   *I'm glad you had your camera.*
- /z/ sounds like /ʒ/   *How was your trip?*

A Mark the linked words in each sentence and check (✓) the pronunciation.

	/tʃ/	/dʒ/	/ʒ/
1. Would you like me to take your coat?	☐	☐	☐
2. I'm not sure what you said.	☐	☐	☐
3. Are you sure he's your tour guide?	☐	☐	☐
4. Why didn't you call me sooner?	☐	☐	☐
5. I forgot to feed your bird.	☐	☐	☐
6. Why did you leave the door open?	☐	☐	☐

B 🎧 **2.19** Listen and check your answers to exercise A. Then listen again and repeat the sentences.

C Work with a partner. Take turns asking and answering these questions. Be sure that you correctly link *you* and *your*.

1. Would you like to go to Tanzania? Why would you or wouldn't you like to go?
2. Is there another migration, human or animal, that you would like to learn more about? Why did you choose that particular migration?
3. If you had the power, would you give tribal peoples special privileges in national parks? What privileges would you give them?
4. Would you believe me if I told you I'm totally dedicated to learning English? Why would you or wouldn't you believe me?
5. When did you last forget your phone somewhere? What did you do?
6. Think about your life last year. Did you have any notable experiences? Did you have any overwhelming ones?
7. Where would you go to put your English to the test? Why would you choose that place?

D ∩ 2.20 Work with a partner. Listen to a wildlife expert explain some of the ways animals find their way when they migrate. Then discuss with your partner whether each statement below is a theory or a fact. Write *Theory* or *Fact*.

CRITICAL THINKING: DISTINGUISHING FACT FROM THEORY

1. _____ Animals migrate mostly for reasons related to basic needs.
2. _____ Some birds use the sun to find their way as they migrate.
3. _____ Some birds use star patterns to choose the direction to travel.
4. _____ Sea turtles use energy patterns to find their way.
5. _____ Many animals use features of the landscape to find their way.
6. _____ Migration directions may be found in the DNA of some animals.

E Work with a partner. Discuss the questions.

CRITICAL THINKING: APPLYING

1. Think of some migrating animals you know about. Describe their migration and the method(s) you think they use to find their way.
2. What are some of the problems migrating animals encounter along the way? Talk about animals that migrate by land, water, and air.
3. How can humans help to solve the problems animals encounter while migrating and allow them to migrate freely and unharmed?

FINAL TASK A Pair Presentation on Animal Migration

> You are going to research information on a migrating animal. Then you will give a pair presentation to the class with the information you researched.

A Work with a partner. Choose a migrating animal that is not in this unit to research. Then follow the steps on the next page.

Monarch butterflies in the Sierra Chincua Sanctuary, Mexico

1. Research basic facts about the animal you chose, including information such as:
   - physical description
   - how long it lives
   - its habitat and range
   - threats it faces

2. Research information about its migration, such as:
   - the migration path
   - the timing of the migration
   - events related to the migration
   - theories and/or facts that explain the migration and how the animals are able to find their way

3. Find a picture of the animal for your presentation.

4. Create a time line of the migration to use as a visual aid for your presentation.

PRESENTATION SKILL Handling Audience Questions

Questions from the audience can be unpredictable. Here's how to handle them:

- Start by saying "Good question!" to be polite and show interest.
- Repeat the question in your own words. This gives you a little extra time, helps you understand the question, and helps the audience understand it.
- Answer the question as clearly as possible. (If you don't know the answer, say something like "I'm afraid I don't have that information right now. I'll have to get back to you later on that." Then research the question and follow up with the person who asked it.)
- Finish by checking if your answer was understood by asking, "Does that make sense?" or "Is that clear?"

ORGANIZING IDEAS **B** With your partner, organize your presentation (using an outline, numbered notes, index cards, etc.). Decide which parts each of you will present. Then practice giving your presentation, including handling audience questions.

PRESENTING **C** Present the information to the class. Answer any questions from your audience. Use the suggestions in the skill box for handling audience questions.

REFLECTION

1. Which information that you learned in this unit is likely to be the most useful to you? Why and how?

_____

_____

2. Which aspect of human or animal migration in this unit did you find the most interesting? Explain.

_____

_____

3. Here are the vocabulary words and phrases from the unit. Check (✓) the ones you can use.

☐ archaeologist	☐ genetic	☐ notable
☐ confront	☐ hypothesis AWL	☐ overwhelming
☐ dedicated to	☐ immense	☐ perspective AWL
☐ descendant	☐ interfere	☐ subsequently AWL
☐ diminish AWL	☐ legislation AWL	☐ tribal
☐ displace AWL	☐ migrate AWL	☐ venture
☐ ecology	☐ monitor AWL	

Independent Student Handbook

Table of Contents

LISTENING SKILLS

Predicting

Speakers giving formal talks usually begin by introducing themselves and their topic. Listen carefully to the introduction of the topic so that you can predict what the talk will be about.

Strategies:

- Use visual information including titles on the board or on presentation slides.
- Think about what you already know about the topic.
- Ask yourself questions that you think the speaker might answer.
- Listen for specific phrases that indicate an introduction (e.g., *My topic is…*).

Listening for Main Ideas

It is important to be able to tell the difference between a speaker's main ideas and supporting details. It is more common for teachers to test understanding of main ideas than of specific details.

Strategies:

- Listen carefully to the introduction. Speakers often state the main idea in the introduction.
- Listen for rhetorical questions, or questions that the speaker asks, and then answers. Often the answer is the statement of the main idea.
- Notice words and phrases that the speaker repeats. Repetition often signals main ideas.

Listening for Details (Examples)

A speaker often provides examples that support a main idea. A good example can help you understand and remember the main idea better.

Strategies:

- Listen for specific phrases that introduce examples.
- Listen for general statements. Examples often follow general statements.

Listening for Details (Cause and Effect)

Speakers often give reasons or list causes and/or effects to support their ideas.

Strategies:

- Notice nouns that might signal causes/reasons (e.g., *factors, influences, causes, reasons*) or effects/results (e.g., *effects, results, outcomes, consequences*).
- Notice verbs that might signal causes/reasons (e.g., *contribute to, affect, influence, determine, produce, result in*) or effects/results (often these are passive, e.g., *is affected by*).

Understanding the Structure of a Presentation

An organized speaker uses expressions to alert the audience to important information that will follow. Recognizing signal words and phrases will help you understand how a presentation is organized and the relationship between ideas.

Introduction

A good introduction identifies the topic and gives an idea of how the lecture or presentation will be organized. Here are some expressions to introduce a topic:

I'll be talking about . . .   *My topic is* . . .

There are basically two groups . . .   *There are three reasons* . . .

Body

In the body of a lecture, speakers usually expand upon the topic. They often use phrases that signal the order of events or subtopics and their relationship to each other. Here are some expressions to help listeners follow the body of a lecture:

The first/next/final (point/reason) is . . .   *First/Next/Finally, let's look at* . . .

Another reason is . . .   *However,* . . .

Conclusion

In the conclusion of a lecture, speakers often summarize what they have said. They may also make predictions or suggestions. Sometimes they ask a question in the conclusion to get the audience to think more about the topic. Here are some expressions to give a conclusion:

In conclusion, . . .   *In summary,* . . .

As you can see. . .   *To review, + (restatement of main points)*

Understanding Meaning from Context

When you are not familiar with a word that a speaker says, you can sometimes guess the meaning of the word or fill in the gaps using the context or situation itself.

Strategies:

- Don't panic. You don't always understand every word of what a speaker says in your first language, either.
- Use context clues to fill in the blanks. What did you understand just before or just after the missing part? What did the speaker probably say?
- Listen for words and phrases that signal a definition or explanation (e.g., *What that means is*…).

Recognizing a Speaker's Bias

Speakers often have an opinion about the topic they are discussing. It's important for you to know if they are objective or subjective about the topic. Objective speakers do not express an opinion. Subjective speakers have a bias or a strong feeling about the topic.

Strategies:

- Notice words like adjectives, adverbs, and modals that the speaker uses (e.g., *ideal, horribly, should, shouldn't*). These suggest that the speaker has a bias.
- Listen to the speaker's voice. Does he or she sound excited, angry, or bored?
- Notice if the speaker gives more weight or attention to one point of view over another.
- Listen for words that signal opinions (e.g., *I think…*).

NOTE-TAKING SKILLS

Taking notes is a personalized skill. It is important to develop a note-taking system that works for you. However, there are some common strategies to improve your note taking.

Before You Listen

Focus

Try to clear your mind before the speaker begins so you can pay attention. If possible, review previous notes or think about what you already know about the topic.

Predict

If you know the topic of the talk, think about what you might hear.

Listen

Take Notes by Hand

Research suggests that taking notes by hand rather than on a computer is more effective. Taking notes by hand requires you to summarize, rephrase, and synthesize information. This helps you *encode* the information, or put it into a form that you can understand and remember.

Listen for Signal Words and Phrases

Speakers often use signal words and phrases (e.g., *Today we're going to talk about…*) to organize their ideas and show relationships between them. Listening for signal words and phrases can help you decide what information to write in your notes.

Condense (Shorten) Information

- As you listen, focus on the most important ideas. The speaker will usually repeat, define, explain, and/or give examples of these ideas. Take notes on these ideas.

    Speaker: *The Itaipu Dam provides about 20% of the electricity used in Brazil and about 75% of the electricity used in Paraguay. That electricity goes to millions of homes and businesses, so it's good for the economy of both countries.*

    Notes: Itaipu Dam → electricity: Brazil 20%, Paraguay 75%

- Don't write full sentences. Write only key words (nouns, verbs, adjectives, and adverbs), phrases, or short sentences.

    Full sentence: *Teachers are normally at the top of the list of happiest jobs.*

    Notes: teachers happiest

- Leave out information that is obvious.

  Full sentence: *Photographer Annie Griffiths is famous for her beautiful photographs. She travels all over the world to take photos.*

  Notes: *A. Griffiths famous for photos; travels world*
- Write numbers and statistics using numerals. (9 bil; 35%)
- Use abbreviations (e.g., *ft., min., yr*) and symbols (=, ≠, >, <, %, →)
- Use indenting. Write main ideas on the left side of the paper. Indent details.
  Benefits of eating ugly foods
     Save $
        10-20% on ugly fruits & vegs. at market
- Write details under key terms to help you remember them.
- Write the definitions of important new words.

After You Listen

- Review your notes soon after the lecture or presentation. Add any details you missed.
- Clarify anything you don't understand in your notes with a classmate or teacher.
- Add or highlight main ideas. Cross out details that aren't important or necessary.
- Rewrite anything that is hard to read or understand. Rewrite your notes in an outline or other graphic organizer to organize the information more clearly.
- Use arrows, boxes, diagrams, or other visual cues to show relationships between ideas.

ORGANIZING INFORMATION

You can use a graphic organizer to take notes while you are listening, or to organize your notes after you listen. Here are some examples of graphic organizers:

Flowcharts are used to show processes, or cause/effect relationships.

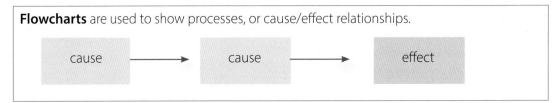

Mind maps show the connection between concepts. The main idea is usually in the center with supporting ideas and details around it.

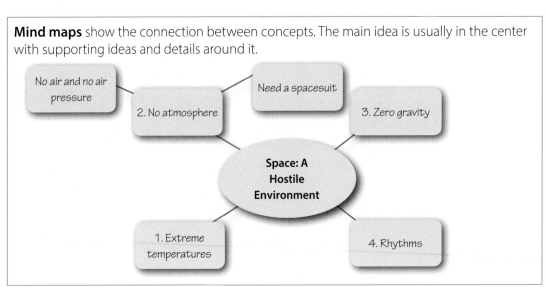

Outlines show the relationship between main ideas and details.

To use an outline for taking notes, write the main ideas at the left margin of your paper. Below the main ideas, indent and write the supporting ideas and details. You may do this as you listen, or go back and rewrite your notes as an outline later.

> **I. Introduction:** How to feed the world
>
> **II. Steps**
>
>   Step One: Stop deforestation
>
>   a. stop burning rainforests
>
>   b. grow crops on land size of South America

T-charts compare two topics.

Climate Change in Greenland	
Benefits	**Drawbacks**
shorter winters	rising sea levels

Timelines show a sequence of events.

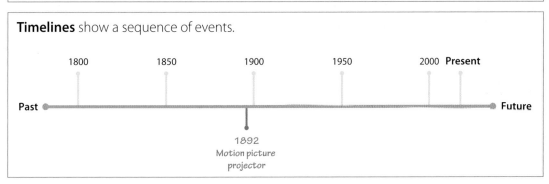

Venn diagrams compare and contrast two or more topics. The overlapping areas show similarities.

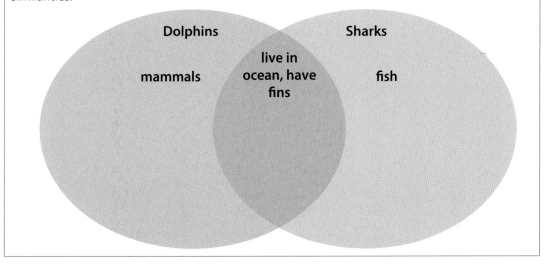

SPEAKING: COMMON PHRASES

Phrases for Expressing Yourself	
Expressing Opinions	**Expressing Likes and Dislikes**
I think…	*I like…*
I believe…	*I prefer…*
I'm sure…	*I love…*
In my opinion/view…	*I can't stand…*
If you ask me,…	*I hate…*
Personally,…	*I really don't like…*
To me,…	*I don't care for…*
Giving Facts	**Giving Tips or Suggestions**
There is evidence/proof…	*Imperatives (e.g., Try to get more sleep.)*
Experts claim/argue…	*You/We should/shouldn't…*
Studies show…	*You/We ought to…*
Researchers found…	*It's (not) a good idea to…*
The record shows…	*I suggest (that)…*
	Let's…
	How about… + (noun/gerund)
	What about… + (noun/gerund)
	Why don't we/you…
	You/We could…
Agreeing	**Disagreeing**
I agree.	*I disagree.*
True.	*I'm not so sure about that.*
Good point.	*I don't know.*
Exactly.	*That's a good point, but I don't agree.*
Absolutely.	*I see what you mean, but I think that…*
I was just about to say that.	
Definitely.	
Right!	

Phrases for Interacting with Others

Clarifying/Checking Your Understanding

So are you saying that…?
So what you mean is…?
What do you mean?
How's that?
How so?
I'm not sure I understand/follow.
Do you mean…?
I'm not sure what you mean.

Asking for Clarification/Confirming Understanding

Sorry, I didn't catch that. Could you repeat it?
I'm not sure I understand the question.
I'm not sure I understand what you mean.
Sorry, I'm not following you.
Are you saying that…?
If I understand correctly, you're saying that…
Oh, now I get it. You're talking about…, right?

Checking Others' Understanding

Does that make sense?
Do you understand?
Do you see what I mean?
Is that clear?
Are you following/with me?
Do you have any questions?

Asking for Opinions

What do you think?
We haven't heard from you in a while.
Do you have anything to add?
What are your thoughts?
How do you feel?
What's your opinion?

Taking Turns

Can/May I say something?
Could I add something?
Can I just say…?
May I continue?
Can I finish what I was saying?
Did you finish your thought?
Let me finish.
Let's get back to…

Interrupting Politely

Excuse me.
Pardon me.
Forgive me for interrupting…
I hate to interrupt but…
Can I stop you for a second?

Asking for Repetition

Could you say that again?
I'm sorry?
I didn't catch what you said.
I'm sorry. I missed that. What did you say?
Could you repeat that please?

Showing Interest

I see.	*Good for you.*
Really?	*Seriously?*
Um-hmm.	*No kidding!*
Wow.	*And? (Then what?)*
That's funny / amazing / incredible / awful!	

SPEAKING: PHRASES FOR PRESENTING

Introduction

Introducing a Topic

I'm going to talk about…
My topic is…
I'm going to present…
I plan to discuss…
Let's start with…

Today we're going to talk about…
So we're going to show you…
Now/Right/So/Well, (pause), let's look at…
*There are three groups/reasons/effects/
factors…*
There are four steps in this process.

Body

Listing or Sequencing

*First/First of all/The first (noun)/To start/To
begin,…*
*Second/Secondly/The second/Next/Another/
Also/Then/In addition,…*
Last/The last/Finally,…
*There are many/several/three types/kinds of/
ways…*

Signaling Problems/Solutions

One problem/issue/challenge is…
One solution/answer/response is…

Giving Reasons or Causes

Because + (clause): *Because the climate is
changing…*
Because of + (noun phrase): *Because of climate
change…*
Due to + (noun phrase)…
Since + (clause)
The reason that I like hip-hop is…
One reason that people listen to music is…
One factor is + (noun phrase)
The main reason that…

Giving Results or Effects

so + (clause): *so I went to the symphony*
Therefore, + (sentence): *Therefore, I went to the
symphony.*
As a result, + (sentence)
Consequently, + (sentence)
…causes + (noun phrase)
…leads to + (noun phrase)
…had an impact/effect on + (noun phrase)
If…then…

Giving Examples

The first example is…
Here's an example of what I mean…
For instance,…
For example,…
Let me give you an example…
…such as…
…like…

Repeating and Rephrasing

What you need to know is…
I'll say this again…
So again, let me repeat…
The most important point is…

Signaling Additional Examples or Ideas	Signaling to Stop Taking Notes
Not only…but,	*You don't need this for the test.*
Besides…	*This information is in your books/on your handout/on the website.*
Not only do…, but also	*You don't have to write all this down.*

Identifying a Side Track	Returning to a Previous Topic
This is off-topic,…	*Getting back to our previous discussion,…*
On a different subject,…	*To return to our earlier topic…*
As an aside, …	*OK, getting back on topic…*
That reminds me…	*So to return to what we were saying,…*

Signaling a Definition	Talking about Visuals
Which means…	*This graph/infographic/diagram shows/explains…*
What that means is…	*The line/box/image represents…*
Or…	*The main point of this visual is…*
In other words,…	*You can see…*
Another way to say that is…	*From this we can see…*
That is…	
That is to say…	

Conclusion

Concluding	
Well/So, that's how I see it.	*To sum up,*
In conclusion,	*As you can see,…*
In summary,	*At the end,…*
	To review, (+ restatement of main points)

PRESENTATION STRATEGIES

You will often have to give individual or group presentations in your class. The strategies below will help you to prepare, present, and reflect on your presentations.

Prepare

As you prepare your presentation:

Consider Your Topic

- **Choose a topic you feel passionate about.** If you are passionate about your topic, your audience will be more interested and excited about your topic, too. Focus on one major idea that you can bring to life. The best ideas are the ones your audience wants to experience.

Consider Your Purpose

- **Have a strong start.** Use an effective hook, such as a quote, an interesting example, a rhetorical question, or a powerful image to get your audience's attention. Include one sentence that explains what you will do in your presentation and why.
- **Stay focused.** Make sure your details and examples support your main points. Avoid sidetracks or unnecessary information that takes you away from your topic.
- **Use visuals that relate to your ideas.** Drawings, photos, video clips, infographics, charts, maps, slides, and physical objects can get your audience's attention and explain ideas effectively. For example, a photo or map of a location you mention can help your audience picture a place they have never been. Slides with only key words and phrases can help emphasize your main points. Visuals should be bright, clear, and simple.
- **Have a strong conclusion.** A strong conclusion should serve the same purpose as a strong start—to get your audience's attention and make them think. Good conclusions often refer back to the introduction, or beginning of the presentation. For example, if you ask a question in the beginning, you can answer it in the conclusion. Remember to restate your main points, and add a conclusion device such as a question, a call to action, or a quote.

Consider your Audience

- **Use familiar concepts.** Think about the people in your audience. Ask yourself these questions: Where are they from? How old are they? What is their background? What do they already know about my topic? What information do I need to explain? Use language and concepts they will understand.
- **Share a personal story.** Consider presenting information that will get an emotional reaction; for example, information that will make your audience feel surprised, curious, worried, or upset. This will help your audience relate to you and your topic.
- **Be authentic (be yourself!).** Write your presentation yourself. Use words that you know and are comfortable using.

Rehearse

- **Make an outline** to help you organize your ideas.
- **Write notes on notecards.** Do not write full sentences, just key words and phrases to help you remember important ideas. Mark the words you should stress and places to pause.
- **Review pronunciation.** Check the pronunciation of words you are uncertain about with a classmate, a teacher, or in a dictionary. Note and practice the pronunciation of difficult words.
- **Memorize the introduction and conclusion.** Rehearse your presentation several times. Practice saying it out loud to yourself (perhaps in front of a mirror or video recorder) and in front of others.
- **Ask for feedback.** Note and revise information that doesn't flow smoothly based on feedback and on your own performance in rehearsal. If specific words or phrases are still a problem, rephrase them.

Present

As you present:

- **Pay attention to your pacing** (how fast or slowly you speak). Remember to speak slowly and clearly. Pause to allow your audience to process information.
- **Speak at a volume loud enough to be heard** by everyone in the audience, but not too loud. Ask the audience if your volume is OK at the beginning of your talk.

- **Vary your intonation.** Don't speak in the same tone throughout the talk. Your audience will be more interested if your voice rises and falls, speeds up and slows down to match the ideas you are talking about.
- **Be friendly and relaxed with your audience**—remember to smile!
- **Show enthusiasm for your topic.** Use humor if appropriate.
- **Have a relaxed body posture.** Don't stand with your arms folded, or look down at your notes. Use gestures when helpful to emphasize your points.
- **Don't read directly from your notes.** Use them to help you remember ideas.
- **Don't look at or read from your visuals too much.** Use them to support your ideas.
- **Make frequent eye contact** with the entire audience.

Reflect

As you reflect on your presentation:

- **Consider what you think went well** during your presentation and what areas you can improve upon.
- **Get feedback** from your classmates and teacher. How do their comments relate to your own thoughts about your presentation? Did they notice things you didn't? How can you use their feedback in your next presentation?

PRESENTATION OUTLINE

When you are planning a presentation, you may find it helpful to use an outline. If it is a group presentation, the outline can provide an easy way to divide the content. For example, one student can do the introduction, another student the first idea in the body, and so on.

1. Introduction

Topic: _____

Hook: _____

Statement of main idea: _____

2. Body

First step/example/reason: _____

    Supporting details: _____ _____ _____

Second step/example/reason: _____

    Supporting details: _____ _____ _____

Third step/example/reason: _____

    Supporting details: _____ _____ _____

3. Conclusion

Main points to summarize: _____ _____

Suggestions/Predictions: _____ _____

Closing comments/summary: _____ _____

PRONUNCIATION GUIDE

Sounds and Symbols

Vowels

Symbol	Key Words
/ɑ/	hot, stop
/æ/	cat, ran
/aɪ/	fine, nice
/i/	eat, need
/ɪ/	sit, him
/eɪ/	name, say
/ɛ/	get, bed
/ʌ/	cup, what
/ə/	about, lesson
/u/	boot, new
/ʊ/	book, could
/oʊ/	go, road
/ɔ/	law, walk
/aʊ/	house, now
/ɔɪ/	toy, coin

Consonants

Symbol	Key Word	Symbol	Key Word
/b/	boy	/t/	tea
/d/	day	/tʃ/	cheap
/dʒ/	job, bridge	/v/	vote
/f/	face	/w/	we
/g/	go	/y/	yes
/h/	hat	/z/	zoo
/k/	key, car		
/l/	love	/ð/	they
/m/	my	/θ/	think
/n/	nine	/ʃ/	shoe
/ŋ/	sing	/ʒ/	measure
/p/	pen		
/r/	right		
/s/	see		

Source: *The Newbury House Dictionary plus Grammar Reference,* Fifth Edition, National Geographic Learning/ Cengage Learning, 2014.

Rhythm

The rhythm of English involves stress and pausing.

Stress

- English words are based on syllables—units of sound that include one vowel sound.

- In every word in English, one syllable has the primary stress.

- In English, speakers group words that go together based on the meaning and context of the sentence. These groups of words are called *thought groups*. In each thought group, one word is stressed more than the others—the stress is placed on the syllable with the primary stress in this word.

- In general, new ideas and information are stressed.

Pausing

- Pauses in English can be divided into two groups: long and short pauses.

- English speakers use long pauses to mark the conclusion of a thought, items in a list, or choices given.

- Short pauses are used in between thought groups to break up the ideas in sentences into smaller, more manageable chunks of information.

English speakers use intonation, or pitch (the rise and fall of their voice), to help express meaning. For example, speakers usually use a rising intonation at the end of *yes/no* questions, and a falling intonation at the end of *wh-* questions and statements.

VOCABULARY BUILDING STRATEGIES

Vocabulary learning is an on-going process. The strategies below will help you learn and remember new vocabulary words.

Guessing Meaning from Context

You can often guess the meaning of an unfamiliar word by looking at or listening to the words and sentences around it. Speakers usually know when a word is unfamiliar to the audience, or is essential to understanding the main ideas, and often provide clues to its meaning.

- Repetition: A speaker may use the same key word or phrase, or use another form of the same word.
- Restatement or synonym: A speaker may give a synonym to explain the meaning of a word, using phrases such as *in other words, also called, or…, also known as.*
- Antonyms: A speaker may define a word by explaining what it is NOT. The speaker may say *Unlike A/In contrast to A, B is…*
- Definition: Listen for signals such as *which means* or *is defined as.* Definitions can also be signaled by a pause.
- Examples: A speaker may provide examples that can help you figure out what something is. For example, *Mascots are a very popular marketing tool. You've seen them on commercials and in ads on social media –* **cute, brightly colored creatures that help sell a product**.

Understanding Word Families: Stems, Prefixes, and Suffixes

Use your understanding of stems, prefixes, and suffixes to recognize unfamiliar words and to expand your vocabulary. The stem is the root part of the word, which provides the main meaning. A prefix comes before the stem and usually modifies meaning (e.g., adding *re-* to a word means "again" or "back"). A suffix comes after the stem and usually changes the part of speech (e.g., adding *-ion, -tion,* or *-ation* to a verb changes it to a noun). Words that share the same stem or root belong to the same word family (e.g., *event, eventful, uneventful, uneventfully*).

Word Stem	Meaning	Example
ann, enn	year	anniversary, millennium
chron(o)	time	chronological, synchronize
flex, flect	bend	flexible, reflection
graph	draw, write	graphics, paragraph
lab	work	labor, collaborate
mob, mot, mov	move	automobile, motivate, mover
port	carry	transport, import
sect	cut	sector, bisect

Prefix	Meaning	Example
dis-	not, opposite of	disappear, disadvantages
in-, im-, il-, ir-	not	inconsistent, immature, illegal, irresponsible
inter-	between	Internet, international
mis-	bad, badly, incorrectly	misunderstand, misjudge
pre-	before	prehistoric, preheat
re-	again; back	repeat; return
trans-	across, beyond	transfer, translate
un-	not	uncooked, unfair

Suffix	Meaning	Example
-able, -ible	worth, ability	believable, impossible
-en	to cause to become; made of	lengthen, strengthen; golden
-er, -or	one who	teacher, director
-ful	full of	beautiful, successful
-ify, -fy	to make or become	simplify, satisfy
-ion, -tion, -ation	condition, action	occasion, education, foundation
-ize	cause	modernize, summarize
-ly	in the manner of	carefully, happily
-ment	condition or result	assignment, statement
-ness	state of being	happiness, sadness

Using a Dictionary

Here are some tips for using a dictionary:

- When you see or hear a new word, try to guess its part of speech (noun, verb, adjective, etc.) and meaning, then look it up in a dictionary.
- Some words have multiple meanings. Look up a new word in the dictionary and try to choose the correct meaning for the context. Then see if it makes sense within the context.
- When you look up a word, look at all the definitions to see if there is a basic core meaning. This will help you understand the word when it is used in a different context. Also look at all the related words, or words in the same family. This can help you expand your vocabulary. For example, the core meaning of *structure* involves something built or put together.

> structure / ˈstrʌktʃər/ *n.* **1** [C] a building of any kind: *A new structure is being built on the corner.* **2** [C] any architectural object of any kind: *The Eiffel Tower is a famous Parisian structure.* **3** [U] the way parts are put together or organized: *the structure of a song‖a business's structure*
> –*v.* [T] **-tured, -turing, -tures** to put together or organize parts of s.t.: *We are structuring a plan to hire new teachers.*
> –*adj.* **structural.**

Source: *The Newbury House Dictionary plus Grammar Reference*, Fifth Edition, National Geographic Learning/Cengage Learning, 2014

Multi-Word Units

You can improve your fluency if you learn and use vocabulary as multi-word units: idioms (*go the extra mile*), collocations (*wide range*), and fixed expressions (*in other words*). Some multi-word units can only be understood as a chunk—the individual words do not add up to the same overall meaning. Keep track of multi-word units in a notebook or on notecards.

Vocabulary Note Cards

You can expand your vocabulary by using vocabulary note cards or a vocabulary building app. Write the word, expression, or sentence that you want to learn on one side. On the other, draw a four-square grid and write the following information in the squares: definition; translation (in your first language); sample sentence; synonyms. Choose words that are high frequency or on the academic word list. If you have looked a word up a few times, you should make a card for it.

definition:	first language translation:
sample sentence:	synonyms:

Organize the cards in review sets so you can practice them. Don't put words that are similar in spelling or meaning in the same review set as you may get them mixed up. Go through the cards and test yourself on the words or expressions. You can also practice with a partner.

VOCABULARY INDEX

Word	Page	CEFR† Level	Word	Page	CEFR† Level	Word	Page	CEFR† Level
posture	154	C1	replicate	114	off-list	tendency	144	C1
practical	54	C1	resistance	184	C2	threaten	24	C1
predator	34	C1	resolve	154	C1	thrive	24	C1
preservation	104	C1	restrict	14	C1	track	154	C2
prey on	34	off-list	retain	64	C2	transaction	134	C1
principle	104	C2	root	194	C1	transition	104	C2
prioritize / prioritise	4	off-list	scarcity	4	C2	tribal	94	C2
			scenario	194	C2	ultimately	114	C1
productivity	154	C1	sector	64	C1	undeniable	34	C1
prominent	74	C2	security	124	C1	undertake	114	C1
promising	64	C1	sedentary	154	C2	unprecedented	174	C2
promote	124	C1	seemingly	134	C1	unquestionably	54	C1
prone to	154	C2	skeptic / sceptic	184	off-list	upkeep	34	C2
pursue	104	C1	spatial	164	off-list	venture	84	C2
radical	174	C1	status	24	C1	verbal	164	C2
random	44	C1	stem from	174	C1	vice versa	164	C1
rank	14	C1	stroll	4	C1	virtue	124	C2
ratio	44	C1	subjective	164	C1	visualize / visualise	164	off-list
regulate	4	C1	subsequently	84	C1			
reluctant	144	C1	substantially	54	C1	well-being	124	C1
reminder	134	C1	superior	174	C1	widespread	64	C1
renovation	4	C1	surge	194	C1	wipe out	24	C2
repetitive	154	C1	sustainable	34	C1	withdraw	134	C1

†The Common European Framework of Reference for Languages (CEFR) is an international standard for describing language proficiency. Pathways Level 4 is intended for students at CEFR level C1. The target vocabulary is at the following CEFR levels:

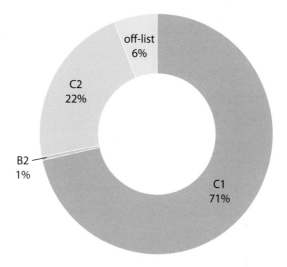

*These words are on the Academic Word List (AWL). The AWL is a list of the 570 highest-frequency academic word families that regularly appear in academic texts. The AWL was compiled by researcher Averil Coxhead based on her analysis of a 3.5-million-word corpus (Coxhead, 2000).

RUBRICS

UNIT 1   Lesson B Lesson Task

Check (✓) if the presenter did the following:	Name		
	_____	_____	_____
1. described a problem affecting a city and its causes	☐	☐	☐
2. proposed possible solutions to the problem	☐	☐	☐
3. used signal phrases to introduce additional aspects of the topic	☐	☐	☐
4. divided the presentation appropriately	☐	☐	☐
5. spoke clearly and at an appropriate pace	☐	☐	☐
6. used appropriate vocabulary	☐	☐	☐
OVERALL RATING Note: 1 = lowest; 5 = highest	1 2 3 4 5	1 2 3 4 5	1 2 3 4 5
Notes:			

UNIT 2   Lesson B Final Task

Check (✓) if the presenters did the following:	Name		
	_____	_____	_____
1. provided appropriate support in favor of or against the argument	☐	☐	☐
2. responded to arguments appropriately	☐	☐	☐
3. debated for three to five minutes	☐	☐	☐
4. spoke clearly and at an appropriate pace	☐	☐	☐
5. used appropriate vocabulary	☐	☐	☐
OVERALL RATING Note: 1 = lowest; 5 = highest	1 2 3 4 5	1 2 3 4 5	1 2 3 4 5
Notes:			

UNIT 3   Lesson B Final Task

Check (✓) if the presenter did the following:	Name		
	_____	_____	_____
1. described fashion trends in a particular location in detail	☐	☐	☐
2. displayed appropriate visuals	☐	☐	☐
3. organized the presentation appropriately	☐	☐	☐
4. paraphrased new or difficult information	☐	☐	☐
5. spoke clearly and at an appropriate pace	☐	☐	☐
6. used appropriate vocabulary	☐	☐	☐
OVERALL RATING Note: 1 = lowest; 5 = highest	1 2 3 4 5	1 2 3 4 5	1 2 3 4 5
Notes:			

UNIT 4   Lesson B Lesson Task

Check (✓) if the presenters did the following:	Name		
	_____	_____	_____
1. described a social media platform and its history	☐	☐	☐
2. discussed the advantages of the platform and how it compares to others	☐	☐	☐
3. evaluated the platform in terms of its effect on globalization and its future prospects	☐	☐	☐
4. clarified terms/ideas with definitions	☐	☐	☐
5. spoke slowly and confidently	☐	☐	☐
6. used appropriate vocabulary	☐	☐	☐
OVERALL RATING Note: 1 = lowest; 5 = highest	1 2 3 4 5	1 2 3 4 5	1 2 3 4 5
Notes:			

UNIT 5   Lesson B Final Task

Check (✓) if the presenters did the following:	Name		
	_____	_____	_____
1. explained the animal migration clearly	☐	☐	☐
2. displayed a time line of the animal migration	☐	☐	☐
3. handled audience questions appropriately	☐	☐	☐
4. spoke clearly and at an appropriate pace	☐	☐	☐
5. used appropriate vocabulary	☐	☐	☐
OVERALL RATING Note: 1 = lowest; 5 = highest	1 2 3 4 5	1 2 3 4 5	1 2 3 4 5
Notes:			

ACKNOWLEDGEMENTS

The Authors and Publisher would like to acknowledge the teachers around the world who participated in the development of the second edition of *Pathways*.

A special thanks to our Advisory Board for their valuable input during the development of this series.

ADVISORY BOARD

Mahmoud Al Hosni, Modern College of Business and Science, Muscat; **Safaa Al-Salim**, Kuwait University, Kuwait City; **Laila AlQadhi**, Kuwait University, Kuwait City; **Julie Bird**, RMIT University Vietnam, Ho Chi Minh City; **Elizabeth Bowles**, Virginia Tech Language and Culture Institute, Blacksburg, VA; **Rachel Bricker**, Arizona State University, Tempe, AZ; **James Broadbridge**, J.F. Oberlin University, Tokyo; **Marina Broeder**, Mission College, Santa Clara, CA; **Shawn Campbell**, Hangzhou High School, Hangzhou; **Trevor Carty**, James Cook University, Singapore; **Jindarat De Vleeschauwer**, Chiang Mai University, Chiang Mai; **Wai-Si El Hassan**, Prince Mohammad Bin Fahd University, Dhahran; **Jennifer Farnell**, University of Bridgeport, Bridgeport, CT; **Rasha Gazzaz**, King Abdulaziz University, Jeddah; **Keith Graziadei**, Santa Monica College, Santa Monica, CA; **Janet Harclerode**, Santa Monica Community College, Santa Monica, CA; **Anna Hasper**, TeacherTrain, Dubai; **Phoebe Kamel Yacob Hindi**, Abu Dhabi Vocational Education and Training Institute, Abu Dhabi; **Kuei-ping Hsu**, National Tsing Hua University, Hsinchu; **Greg Jewell**, Drexel University, Philadelphia, PA; **Adisra Katib**, Chulalongkorn University Language Institute, Bangkok; **Wayne Kennedy**, LaGuardia Community College, Long Island City, NY; **Beth Koo**, Central Piedmont Community College, Charlotte, NC; **Denise Kray**, Bridge School, Denver, CO; **Chantal Kruger**, ILA Vietnam, Ho Chi Minh City; **William P. Kyzner**, Fuyang AP Center, Fuyang; **Becky Lawrence**, Massachusetts International Academy, Marlborough, MA; **Deborah McGraw**, Syracuse University, Syracuse, NY; **Mary Moore**, University of Puerto Rico, San Juan; **Raymond Purdy**, ELS Language Centers, Princeton, NJ; **Anouchka Rachelson**, Miami Dade College, Miami, FL; **Fathimah Razman**, Universiti Utara Malaysia, Sintok; **Phil Rice**, University of Delaware ELI, Newark, DE; **Scott Rousseau**, American University of Sharjah, Sharjah; **Verna Santos-Nafrada**, King Saud University, Riyadh; **Eugene Sidwell**, American Intercon Institute, Phnom Penh; **Gemma Thorp**, Monash University English Language Centre, Melbourne; **Matt Thurston**, University of Central Lancashire, Preston; **Christine Tierney**, Houston Community College, Houston, TX; **Jet Robredillo Tonogbanua**, FPT University, Hanoi.

GLOBAL REVIEWERS

ASIA

Antonia Cavcic, Asia University, Tokyo; **Soyhan Egitim**, Tokyo University of Science, Tokyo; **Caroline Handley**, Asia University, Tokyo; **Patrizia Hayashi**, Meikai University, Urayasu; **Greg Holloway**, University of Kitakyushu, Kitakyushu; **Anne C. Ihata**, Musashino University, Tokyo; **Kathryn Mabe**, Asia University, Tokyo; **Frederick Navarro Bacala**, Yokohama City University, Yokohama; **Tyson Rode**, Meikai University, Urayasu; **Scott Shelton-Strong**, Asia University, Tokyo; **Brooks Slaybaugh**, Yokohama City University, Yokohama; **Susanto Sugiharto**, Sutomo Senior High School, Medan; **Andrew Zitzmann**, University of Kitakyushu, Kitakyushu

LATIN AMERICA AND THE CARIBBEAN

Raul Billini, ProLingua, Dominican Republic; **Alejandro Garcia**, Collegio Marcelina, Mexico; **Humberto Guevara**, Tec de Monterrey, Campus Monterrey, Mexico; **Romina Olga Planas**, Centro Cultural Paraguayo Americano, Paraguay; **Carlos Rico-Troncoso**, Pontificia Universidad Javeriana, Colombia; **Ialê Schetty**, Enjoy English, Brazil; **Aline Simoes**, Way To Go Private English, Brazil; **Paulo Cezar Lira Torres**, APenglish, Brazil; **Rosa Enilda Vasquez**, Swisher Dominicana, Dominican Republic; **Terry Whitty**, LDN Language School, Brazil.

MIDDLE EAST AND NORTH AFRICA

Susan Daniels, Kuwait University, Kuwait; **Mahmoud Mohammadi Khomeini**, Sokhane Ashna Language School, Iran; **Müge Lenbet**, Koç University, Turkey; **Robert Anthony Lowman**, Prince Mohammad bin Fahd University, Saudi Arabia; **Simon Mackay**, Prince Mohammad bin Fahd University, Saudi Arabia.

USA AND CANADA

Frank Abbot, Houston Community College, Houston, TX; **Hossein Aksari**, Bilingual Education Institute and Houston Community College, Houston, TX; **Sudie Allen-Henn**, North Seattle College, Seattle, WA; **Sharon Allie**, Santa Monica Community College, Santa Monica, CA; **Jerry Archer**, Oregon State University, Corvallis, OR; **Nicole Ashton**, Central Piedmont Community College, Charlotte, NC; **Barbara Barrett**, University of Miami, Coral Gables, FL; **Maria Bazan-Myrick**, Houston Community College, Houston, TX; **Rebecca Beal**, Colleges of Marin, Kentfield, CA; **Marlene Beck**, Eastern Michigan University, Ypsilanti, MI; **Michelle Bell**, University of Southern California, Los Angeles, CA; **Linda Bolet**, Houston Community College, Houston, TX; **Jenna Bollinger**, Eastern Michigan University, Ypsilanti, MI; **Monica Boney**, Houston Community College, Houston, TX; **Nanette Bouvier**, Rutgers University – Newark, Newark, NJ; **Nancy Boyer**, Golden West College, Huntington Beach, CA; **Lia Brenneman**, University of Florida English Language Institute, Gainesville, FL; **Colleen Brice**, Grand Valley State University, Allendale, MI; **Kristen Brown**, Massachusetts International Academy, Marlborough, MA; **Philip Brown**, Houston Community

College, Houston, TX; **Dongmei Cao**, San Jose City College, San Jose, CA; **Molly Cheney**, University of Washington, Seattle, WA; **Emily Clark**, The University of Kansas, Lawrence, KS; **Luke Coffelt**, International English Center, Boulder, CO; **William C Cole-French**, MCPHS University, Boston, MA; **Charles Colson**, English Language Institute at Sam Houston State University, Huntsville, TX; **Lucy Condon**, Bilingual Education Institute, Houston, TX; **Janice Crouch**, Internexus Indiana, Indianapolis, IN; **Charlene Dandrow**, Virginia Tech Language and Culture Institute, Blacksburg, VA; **Loretta Davis**, Coastline Community College, Westminster, CA; **Marta Dmytrenko-Ahrabian**, Wayne State University, Detroit, MI; **Bonnie Duhart**, Houston Community College, Houston, TX; **Karen Eichhorn**, International English Center, Boulder, CO; **Tracey Ellis**, Santa Monica Community College, Santa Monica, CA; **Jennifer Evans**, University of Washington, Seattle, WA; **Marla Ewart**, Bilingual Education Institute, Houston, TX; **Rhoda Fagerland**, St. Cloud State University, St. Cloud, MN; **Kelly Montijo Fink**, Kirkwood Community College, Cedar Rapids, IA; **Celeste Flowers**, University of Central Arkansas, Conway, AR; **Kurtis Foster**, Missouri State University, Springfield, MO; **Rachel Garcia**, Bilingual Education Institute, Houston, TX; **Thomas Germain**, University of Colorado Boulder, Boulder, CO; **Claire Gimble**, Virginia International University, Fairfax, VA; **Marilyn Glazer-Weisner**, Middlesex Community College, Lowell, MA; **Amber Goodall**, South Piedmont Community College, Charlotte, NC; **Katya Goussakova**, Seminole State College of Florida, Sanford, FL; **Jane Granado**, Texas State University, San Marcos, TX; **Therea Hampton**, Mercer County Community College, West Windsor Township, NJ; **Jane Hanson**, University of Nebraska – Lincoln, Lincoln, NE; **Lauren Heather**, University of Texas at San Antonio, San Antonio, TX; **Jannette Hermina**, Saginaw Valley State University, Saginaw, MI; **Gail Hernandez**, College of Staten Island, Staten Island, NY; **Beverly Hobbs**, Clark University, Worcester, MA; **Kristin Homuth**, Language Center International, Southfield, MI; **Tim Hooker**, Campbellsville University, Campbellsville, KY; **Raylene Houck**, Idaho State University, Pocatello, ID; **Karen L. Howling**, University of Bridgeport, Bridgeport, CT; **Sharon Jaffe**, Santa Monica Community College, Santa Monica, CA; **Andrea Kahn**, Santa Monica Community College, Santa Monica, CA; **Eden Bradshaw Kaiser**, Massachusetts International Academy, Marlborough, MA; **Mandy Kama**, Georgetown University, Washington, D.C.; **Andrea Kaminski**, University of Michigan – Dearborn, Dearborn, MI; **Phoebe Kang**, Brock University, Ontario; **Eileen Kramer**, Boston University CELOP, Brookline, MA; **Rachel Lachance**, University of New Hampshire, Durham, NH; **Janet Langon**, Glendale Community College, Glendale, CA; **Frances Le Grand**, University of Houston, Houston, TX; **Esther Lee**, California State University, Fullerton, CA; **Helen S. Mays Lefal**, American Learning Institute, Dallas, TX; **Oranit Limmaneeprasert**, American River College, Sacramento, CA; **Dhammika Liyanage**, Bilingual Education Institute, Houston, TX; **Emily Lodmer**, Santa Monica Community College, Santa Monica Community College, CA; **Ari Lopez**, American Learning Institute Dallas, TX; **Nichole Lukas**, University of Dayton, Dayton, OH; **Undarmaa Maamuujav**, California State University, Los Angeles, CA; **Diane Mahin**, University of Miami, Coral Gables, FL; **Melanie Majeski**, Naugatuck Valley Community College, Waterbury, CT; **Judy Marasco**, Santa Monica Community College, Santa Monica, CA; **Murray McMahan**, University of Alberta, Alberta; **Deirdre McMurtry**, University of Nebraska Omaha, Omaha, NE; **Suzanne Meyer**, University of Pittsburgh, Pittsburgh, PA; **Cynthia Miller**, Richland College, Dallas, TX; **Sara Miller**, Houston Community College, Houston, TX; **Gwendolyn Miraglia**, Houston Community College, Houston, TX; **Katie Mitchell**, International English Center, Boulder, CO; **Ruth Williams Moore**, University of Colorado Boulder, Boulder, CO; **Kathy Najafi**, Houston Community College, Houston, TX; **Sandra Navarro**, Glendale Community College, Glendale, CA; **Stephanie Ngom**, Boston University, Boston MA; **Barbara Niemczyk**, University of Bridgeport, Bridgeport, CT; **Melody Nightingale**, Santa Monica Community College, Santa Monica, CA; **Alissa Olgun**, California Language Academy, Los Angeles, CA; **Kimberly Oliver**, Austin Community College, Austin, TX; **Steven Olson**, International English Center, Boulder, CO; **Fernanda Ortiz**, University of Arizona, Tucson, AZ; **Joel Ozretich**, University of Washington, Seattle, WA; **Erin Pak**, Schoolcraft College, Livonia, MI; **Geri Pappas**, University of Michigan – Dearborn, Dearborn, MI; **Eleanor Paterson**, Erie Community College, Buffalo, NY; **Sumeeta Patnaik**, Marshall University, Huntington, WV; **Mary Peacock**, Richland College, Dallas, TX; **Kathryn Porter**, University of Houston, Houston, TX; **Eileen Prince**, Prince Language Associates, Newton Highlands, MA; **Marina Ramirez**, Houston Community College, Houston, TX; **Laura Ramm**, Michigan State University, East Lansing, MI; **Chi Rehg**, University of South Florida, Tampa, FL; **Cyndy Reimer**, Douglas College, New Westminster, British Columbia; **Sydney Rice**, Imperial Valley College, Imperial, CA; **Lynnette Robson**, Mercer University, Macon, GA; **Helen E. Roland**, Miami Dade College, Miami, FL; **Maria Paula Carreira Rolim**, Southeast Missouri State University, Cape Girardeau, MO; **Jill Rolston-Yates**, Texas State University, San Marcos, TX; **David Ross**, Houston Community College, Houston, TX; **Rachel Scheiner**, Seattle Central College, Seattle, WA; **John Schmidt**, Texas Intensive English Program, Austin, TX; **Mariah Schueman**, University of Miami, Coral Gables, FL; **Erika Shadburne**, Austin Community College, Austin, TX; **Mahdi Shamsi**, Houston Community College, Houston, TX; **Osha Sky**, Highline College, Des Moines, WA; **William Slade**, University of Texas, Austin, TX; **Takako Smith**, University of Nebraska – Lincoln, Lincoln, NE; **Barbara Smith-Palinkas**, Hillsborough Community College, Tampa, FL; **Paula Snyder**, University of Missouri, Columbia, MO; **Mary; Evelyn Sorrell**, Bilingual Education Institute, Houston TX; **Kristen Stauffer**, International English Center, Boulder, CO; **Christina Stefanik**, The Language Company, Toledo, OH; **Cory Stewart**, University of Houston, Houston, TX; **Laurie Stusser-McNeill**, Highline College, Des Moines, WA; **Tom Sugawara**, University of Washington, Seattle, WA; **Sara Sulko**, University of Missouri, Columbia, MO; **Mark Sullivan**, University of Colorado Boulder, Boulder, CO; **Olivia Szabo**, Boston University, Boston, MA; **Amber Tallent**, University of Nebraska Omaha, Omaha, NE; **Amy Tate**, Rice University, Houston, USA; **Aya C. Tiacoh**, Bilingual Education Institute, Houston, TX; **Troy Tucker**, Florida SouthWestern State College, Fort Myers, FL; **Anne Tyoan**, Savannah College of Art and Design, Savannah, GA; **Michael Vallee**, International English Center, Boulder, CO; **Andrea Vasquez**, University of Southern Maine, Portland, ME; **Jose Vasquez**, University of Texas Rio Grande Valley, Edinburg, TX; **Maureen Vendeville**, Savannah Technical College, Savannah, GA; **Melissa Vervinck**, Oakland University, Rochester, MI; **Adriana Villarreal**, Universided Nacional Autonoma de Mexico, San Antonio, TX; **Summer Webb**, International English Center, Boulder, CO; **Mercedes Wilson-Everett**, Houston Community College, Houston, TX; **Lora Yasen**, Tokyo International University of America, Salem, OR; **Dennis Yommer**, Youngstown State University, Youngstown, OH; **Melojeane (Jolene) Zawilinski**, University of Michigan – Flint, Flint, MI.

CREDITS

Photos

Cover Credit: Guang Niu/Getty Images
1 (t) 2009 TYRONE TURNER/National Geographic Image Collection, **2-3** (c) Kirklandphotos/Getty Images, (t) Cengage Learning, Inc., **5** (b) Alan Tan Photography/Shutterstock.com, **6** (c) ©National Geographic Maps, (bl) Franco Debernardi/Getty Images, **9** (br) Cengage Learning, Inc., (bl) USGS, 010-011 (b) mandritoiu/Shutterstock.com, **12** (t) VCG/Getty Images, **15** (t) DESIGN PICS INC/National Geographic Creative, **16** (cl) ©National Geographic Maps, (b) DESIGN PICS INC/National Geographic Creative, **19** (t) FRANCOIS GUILLOT/Getty Images, **21** (t) ©Brent Stirton/Reportage/Getty Images, **22** (l) AFP/Getty Images, **23** (r) ©Joel Sartore/National Geographic Photo Ark, **24** (b) Francois Gohier/VWPics/Alamy, **26** (tr) Science History Images/Alamy, **28** (b) PAUL NICKLEN/National Geographic Creative, **31** (c) Heather Lucia Snow/Shutterstock, **32** (t) ©Axel Gomille/NPL/Minden Pictures, **34** (b) ROBBIE GEORGE/National Geographic Creative, **36** (b) Edwin Remsberg/Alamy Stock Photo, **39** (b) Charles Mostoller/Reuters, **41** (t) Tristan Fewings/Getty Images, **42-43** (t) Anadolu Agency/Getty Images, **43** (r) Cengage Learning, Inc., **44** (tr) Tim Graham/Alamy Stock Photo, **46** (c) RightsLink, **49** (b) JODI COBB/National Geographic creative, **50** (t) ©Xavier Zimbardo/Getty Images, **52** (t) SARAH LEEN/National Geographic Creative, **53** (b) www.BibleLandPictures.com/Alamy Stock Photo, **54** (tr) Camila Turriani/Alamy Stock Photo, **56** (tl) ©Alex Soza, (cl) Tom Vickers/Newscom/Splash News/Ventura/CA/United States, (cl) Chung Sung-Jun/Getty Images, **60** (t) Alexey Kopytko/Getty Images, 61 (c) ©Marla Aufmuth/TED, **62-63** (c) © Matthew Mahon/Redux Pictures, (c) Daxiao Productions/Shutterstock.com, **66** (b) Grapheast/Alamy Stock Photo, **69** (c) ©National Geographic Maps, (b) ©National Geographic Maps, **71** (b) ©Mark Leong/Redux, 72 (t) ©Aaron Huey/National Geographic Creative, (tl) National Geographic, **74** (cr) Oliver Uberti/National Geographic Magazine, **75** (b) Meldmedia Inc., **76** (c) Oliver Uberti/National Geographic Creative, 81 (c) JOE RIIS/National Geographic Creative, **82-83** (c) Morris Ryan/National Geographic Creative, (c) John Stanmeyer LLC/National Geographic Creative, **84** (tl) Cengage Learning, Inc., **86** (t) MARK THIESSEN/National Geographic, **88** (b) Gregory Manchess/National Geographic Creative, **90** (b) ©Stephen Alvarez/National Geographic Creative, **92** (t) Frans Lanting/National Geographic Creative, (cr) Cengage Learning, Inc., **94** (cl) Martin Gamache/National Geographic Creative, **95** (b) Jonathan Eden/Alamy, **97** (b) MICHAEL NICHOLS/National Geographic Creative, **99** (b) JOEL SARTORE/National Geographic Creative.

Maps

2-3 Created by MPS; **6** Mapping Specialists; **16** Mapping Specialists; **69** Adapted from "Interconnectivity," National Geographic Maps, 2014; **82-83** Adapted from "The Longest Walk," National Geographic, December 2013; **84** Adapted from "Early Americans," https://mrgrayhistory.wikispaces.com/UNIT+8+-+EARLY+AMERICAS; **92** Mapping Specialists; Map courtesy of Roy Safaris–Tanzania; **94** Adapted from "Who Owns This Land?" by Martin Gamache and Lauren C. Tierney, National Geographic, May 2016.

Illustrations/Infographics

2-3 "The 10 Most Multicultural Cities In The World," https://theculturetrip.com/north-america/usa/california/articles/the-10-most-multicultural-cities-in-the-world/; "The 10 Most Visited Cities of 2017," http://www.cntraveler.com/galleries/2015-06-03/the-10-most-visited-cities-of-2015-london-bangkok-new-york/10 **9** Adapted from "Can Venice be Saved?" https://sites.google.com/site/unknownglobalhazards/subsidence-in-venice/why-is-subsidence-a-problem; **23** Adapted from "Meet Some of the Species Facing Extinction in the Wild," National Geographic/Joel Sartore, Photo Ark; **39** Adapted from "Saving Wildlife Through Licenses and Taxes," National Geographic, November 2007; **43** Adapted from "Top 3 Reasons for Trying to Look Good and Weekly Time Spent on Personal Grooming," https://blog.gfk.com/2016/01/what-makes-us-want-to-look-good/; **48** Adapted from "Countries with Top Number of Procedures, 2010," National Geographic, December 2012; **63** Adapted from "Future Work Skills 2020," http://www.iftf.org/futureworkskills/; **64** Adapted from "Net Employment Outlook by Job Family, 2015-2020," http://reports.weforum.org/future-of-jobs-2016/employment-trends/; **74** Adapted from "Revealed World," National Geographic, September 2010; **76** "Revealed World," National Geographic, September 2010; **79** Adapted from "Active Users of Key Global Social Platforms," https://wearesocial.com/special-reports/digital-in-2017-global-overview.

Listening and Text Sources

6-8 "Vanishing Venice" by Cathy Newman, National Geographic, August 2009; "Venice Tourism Debate 2015: Residents Fear Visitors Are Destroying Their City, Demand Authorities Crack Down On Cruise Ships," http://www.ibtimes.com/venice-tourism-debate-2015-residents-fear-visitors-are-destroying-their-city-demand-2063682; "Venice Matters to History – Ventians Matter to Me," http://news.nationalgeographic.com/news/2015/01/150129-venice-my-town-zwingle-grand-canal-motondoso-piazza-san-marco-vaporetto/; **14** "10 Most Affluent Cities In The World: Macau and Hartford Top The List," http://www.newgeography.com/content/004853-10-most-affluent-cities-world-macau-and-hartford-top-list; "List of countries and dependencies by area," https://en.wikipedia.org/wiki/List_of_countries_and_dependencies_by_area; "Singapore," http://www.averagesalarysurvey.com/singapore; **16-17** "The Singapore Solution," by Mark Jacobson, National Geographic, January 2010; **17** "16 Odd Things that are Illegal in Singapore," http://www.businessinsider.com/things-that-are-illegal-in-singapore-2015-7; "$200 Fine for Anyone Caught Breeding Mozzies," http://www.straitstimes.com/singapore/health/200-fine-for-anyone-caught-breeding-mozzies **24** "Species Guide," http://us.whales.org/species-guide?gclid=Cj0KCQjwn6DMBRC0ARIsAHZtCeON4EPNKq59YzOdMc1XIQ0VABitwoyoKCAzJsrdXKxryetvrdqJvUYaAtpFEALw_wcB; "U.S. Leads New Bid to Phase Out Whale Hunting," http://www.nytimes.com/2010/04/15/science/earth/15whale.html?_r=1&; **25** "International Convention for the Regulation of Whaling," https://en.wikipedia.org/wiki/International_Convention_for_the_Regulation_of_Whaling; "Which Cetacean Species are Extinct?" http://baleinesendirect.org/en/which-cetacean-species-are-extinct/; "British Adventurer Builds Whale-shaped Boat to Sail to Canada," http://www.cbc.ca/radio/asithappens/as-it-happens-wednesday-edition-1.3472671/british-adventurer-builds-whale-shaped-boat-to-sail-to-canada-1.3472704; **26-27** "Last One" by Verlyn Klinkenborg, National Geographic, January 2009; "Listed Species Summary (Boxscore)," http://ecos.fws.gov/ecp0/reports/box-score-report; **34** "Wolf Wars" by Douglas Chadwick, National Geographic, March 2010; **36-38** "Hunters: For the Love of the Land," by Robert M. Poole, National Geographic, November 2007; **46** "New 'Golden' Ratios for Facial Beauty" by Pamela M. Pallett, Stephen Link, and Kang Lee, https://www.ncbi.nlm.nih.gov/pmc/articles/PMC2814183/; **46-47, 49** "The Enigma of Beauty" by Cathy Newman, National Geographic, January 2000; **56-57** "Dreamweavers" by Cathy Newman, National Geographic, January 2003; "Artificial Spider Silk Could Be Used for Armor, More" by Brian Handwerk, National Geographic Daily News, January 14, 2005; **67** "What Skills We Need to Succeed in the World," YouTube, posted by Globalization 101, August 23, 2010; WESO Trends 2017: The Disconnect Between Growth and Employment," http://www.ilo.org/global/about-the-ilo/multimedia/video/institutional-videos/WCMS_541539/lang--en/index.htm; "Decision-making with Emotional Intelligence," https://www.ideasforleaders.com/ideas/decision-making-with-emotional-intelligence; **68** "Globalization Terminology," https://en.wikipedia.org/wiki/Category:Globalization_terminology; **74** "Revealed World" by Tim Folger, National Geographic, September 2010; **76-77** "Is Pokémon Go Taking Over the World?", https://kantanmtblog.com/2016/07/25/is-pokemon-go-taking-over-the-world/; "Pokémon Go Becomes Global Craze as Game Overtakes Twitter for US Users," https://www.theguardian.com/technology/2016/jul/12/pokemon-go-becomes-global-phenomenon-as-number-of-us-users-overtakes-twitter; "Popular Augmented

Reality & Pokémon Go! Shows," https://www.mixcloud.com/discover/augmented-reality+pokemon-go/; "Virtual and Augmented Reality Could Take Online Meetings to the Next Level," http://blog.clickmeeting.com/virtual-and-augmented-reality-could-take-online-meetings-to-the-next-level; "Deglobalization is Already Well Underway – Here are 4 Technologies that Will Speed it Up," http://www.mauldineconomics.com/editorial/deglobalization-is-already-well-underwayhere-are-4-technologies-that-will-s; **84** "Tracking the First Americans" by Glenn Hodges, National Geographic, January 2015; **86–88** "The Greatest Journey: The Trail of Our DNA," by James Shreeve, National Geographic, March 2006; "From Africa to Astoria by Way of Everywhere" by James Shreeve, http://ngm.nationalgeographic.com/big-idea/02/queens-genes, August 17, 2009; **94** Adapted from "Who Owns This Land?" by Martin Gamache and Lauren C. Tierney, National Geographic, May 2016; **96–97** "Heartbreak on the Serengeti" by Robert M. Poole, National Geographic, February 2006; **99** "Animal Migration: Facts," idahoptv.org/sciencetrek/topics/animal_migration/facts.cfm.

INDEX OF EXAM SKILLS AND TASKS

Pathways Listening, Speaking, and Critical Thinking is designed to provide practice for standardized exams, such as IELTS and TOEFL. Many activities in this book practice or focus on the **key exam skills** needed for test success. In addition, a number of activities are designed to be the same as (or similar to) **common question types** found in these tests and to provide effective practice of these questions.

Listening

Key Exam Skills	IELTS	TOEFL	Page(s) / Exercise(s)
Distinguishing facts from theories	X	X	86 LS, 87 C, 99 D
Listening for advantages	X	X	66 LS, 67 C
Listening for clarifying answers	X	X	96 LS, 97 D
Listening for key details or specific information	X	X	56 LS, 56 C, 77 C, 96 C, 107 C, 127 C, 137 C, 167 C, 177 D, 197 D
Listening for main ideas	X	X	7 C, 46 B, 56 B, 76 B, 96 B, 106 B, 126 B, 136 B, 146 C, 156 B, 157 D, 166 B, 186 B, 196 B
Listening for positive or negative views	X	X	157 LS, 157 C
Listening for shifts in topic	X	X	137 LS
Taking notes: using abbreviations	X	X	7 NT, 7 D, 7 E
Taking notes: using a time line or idea map	X	X	87 NT, 87 D, 107 NT, 107 D, 117 D
Taking notes: using a T-chart	X	X	146 NT, 147 D
Understanding the introduction to a lecture	X	X	6 LS, 6 B
Using prior knowledge to listen effectively	X	X	36 LS, 36 A, 66 A, 96 A, 146 A, 156 A, 166 A, 196 A

KEY

EL — Everyday Language
LS — Listening Skill
NT — Note-Taking Skill
PRON — Pronunciation
SS — Speaking Skill

Common Question Types	IELTS	TOEFL	Page(s) / Exercise(s)
Connecting content		X	146 C, 156 B, 166 B, 186 B
Matching	X		46 B, 137 D, 168 A
Multiple choice	X	X	6 B, 126 B
Multiple response		X	6 C, 76 B, 106 B, 136 B
Note completion	X		7 D, 27 D, 27 E, 47 C, 57 D, 67 C, 77 C, 87 D, 107 D, 117 D, 127 C, 147 D, 167 C, 177 E, 187 C, 187 D
Sentence completion	X		17 D
Short answer	X		177 D, 197 D

INDEX OF EXAM SKILLS AND TASKS

Speaking

KEY

EL	Everyday Language
LS	Listening Skill
NT	Note-Taking Skill
PRON	Pronunciation
SS	Speaking Skill

Pathways	CEFR	IELTS Band	TOEFL Score
Level 4	**C1**	**6.5–7.0**	**81–100**
Level 3	B2	5.5–6.0	51–80
Level 2	B1–B2	4.5–5.0	31–50
Level 1	A2–B1	0–4.0	0–30
Foundations	A1–A2		